COUNTRIES OF THE WORLD

USA

Gareth Stevens Publishing
A WORLD ALMANAC EDUCATION GROUP COMPANY

About the Author: Elizabeth Berg lives and works in the United States. She has extensive experience as a freelance writer and has written and edited many children's books.

PICTURE CREDITS
Bes Stock: 23, 24, 45, 65
Camera Press: 14, 16, 30, 61, 63, 72, 75, 78, 80, 85
Focus Team: Cover, 3 (center), 22, 43, 64, 74
Haga Library: 1, 21, 32 (bottom), 35, 39 (both), 52, 53
Blaine Harrington: 6, 20, 25, 36, 37, 91
HBL Network: 11 (bottom), 13, 17, 18, 29 (top), 32 (top), 44, 47, 49, 55 (left), 66, 67 (both), 71, 77 (both), 79, 82
Dave G. Houser: 3 (top), 5, 8 (top), 9 (both), 10, 19, 48, 57, 83
The Hutchison Library: 26, 27, 31 (bottom), 33, 34, 60, 70
International Photobank: 2, 4, 7, 8 (bottom), 42, 51, 73, 84
Network Photo Agency: 81
North Wind Picture Archives: 3 (bottom), 15 (all), 28, 29 (bottom), 58, 62, 68, 69, 76
Christine Osborne: 38, 40, 41 (both)
Times Editions: 90 (both)
Topham Picturepoint: 31 (top), 55 (right)
Vision Photo Agency: 12, 46
Horst Von Irmer: 11 (top), 50, 54, 56, 59

Digital Scanning by Superskill Graphics Pte Ltd

Written by
ELIZABETH BERG

Edited by
ELLEN WHITE

Designed by
LOO CHUAN MING

Picture research by
THOMAS KHOO

Updated and reprinted in 2005.
First published in North America in 1999 by
Gareth Stevens Publishing
A World Almanac Education Group Company
330 West Olive Street, Suite 100
Milwaukee, Wisconsin 53212 USA

Please visit our web site at:
www.garethstevens.com
For a free color catalog describing
Gareth Stevens' list of high-quality books
and multimedia programs, call
1-800-542-25925 (USA) or
1-800-387-3178 (CANADA).
Gareth Stevens Publishing's
Fax: (414) 332-3567.

© **TIMES EDITIONS PTE LTD 1999**
© **MARSHALL CAVENDISH INT'L (ASIA) PRIVATE LIMITED 2005**
Originated and designed by Times Editions–Marshall Cavendish
An imprint of Marshall Cavendish International (Asia) Private Limited
A member of Times Publishing Limited
Times Centre, 1 New Industrial Road
Singapore 536196
http://www.marshallcavendish.com/genref

Library of Congress Cataloging-in-Publication Data
Berg, Elizabeth. 1953–
USA / by Elizabeth Berg.
p. cm. -- (Countries of the world)
Includes bibliographical references and index.
Summary: An overview of the United States of America that includes information on geography, history, government, lifestyle, language, customs, and current issues.
ISBN 0-8368-2313-3 (lib. bdg.)
1. United States--Juvenile literature. [1. United States.] I. Title.
II. Series: Countries of the world (Milwaukee, Wis.)
E156.B47   1999
973--dc21   98-52427

Printed in Singapore

3 4 5 6 7 8 9 05

Contents

5 AN OVERVIEW OF THE USA

6   Geography
10   History
16   Government and the Economy
20   People and Lifestyle
28   Language and Literature
30   Arts
34   Leisure and Festivals
40   Food

43 A CLOSER LOOK AT THE USA

44   Basketball
46   Civil Rights
48   Cowboys
50   The Everglades
52   Halloween
54   Hollywood
56   The Mississippi River
58   Native Americans
60   Puerto Rico
62   Quakers and Shakers
64   The Redwoods
66   Rock 'n' Roll
68   Rushing for Gold
70   Skyscrapers
72   To the Moon

75 FOREIGN RELATIONS

For More Information ...
86   Full-color map
88   Black-and-white reproducible map
90   USA at a Glance
92   Glossary
94   Books, Videos, Web Sites
95   Index

AN OVERVIEW OF THE USA

The United States is a country of contrasts: of snow-covered peaks and sprawling deserts, of densely packed cities and uninhabited wilderness, of enormous riches and terrible poverty. It includes some of the coldest, hottest, driest, wettest, and windiest places on Earth. The sheer size of the United States has been an important influence on how Americans think and act. Throughout the country's history, there has been a new frontier for Americans to explore, whether in science and technology, world politics, or the arts. The hard work and pioneering spirit of immigrants from every corner of the world helped build the country and create a melting pot of races and ethnic groups.

Opposite: **San Francisco is a port in northern California. It is famous for its trolley cars, the Golden Gate Bridge, and the island of Alcatraz, located in the middle of the bay. Alcatraz was once the site of a famous prison.**

Below: **Camping and fishing are popular American pastimes.**

THE FLAG OF THE UNITED STATES

Often referred to as the Stars and Stripes, the American flag was adopted in 1776 when the country declared its independence. Legend has it that Betsy Ross (1752–1836), a Philadelphia flagmaker, made the first flag. This, however, has never been proven. The thirteen red and white stripes represent the original thirteen colonies. The fifty white stars represent the total number of states in the Union — the original thirteen plus territories annexed after 1776. Hawaii, the fiftieth state, was annexed on August 21, 1959. The configuration of stars changed over the years, first appearing in a circle and then in rows.

Geography

The United States is the fourth largest country in the world and includes a wide range of terrain and climates. It is made up of fifty states, including Alaska, which lies to the north of Canada, and Hawaii, an archipelago in the Pacific Ocean. The forty-eight states in North America occupy an area of 3,787,300 square miles (9,809,107 square kilometers) bound by the Atlantic and Pacific Oceans, the Canadian border, and Mexico.

Forested coastal plains border the eastern seaboard, ending at the lower slopes of the Appalachian Mountains, which extend from Alabama to Maine. To the west of the Appalachians are the great central plains. Originally vast prairies filled with herds of wild buffalo, the plains are now the country's farm belt, where wheat and corn are grown. The central plains end at the foothills of the Rocky Mountains, which stretch from New Mexico to Canada and Alaska. The soaring peaks of the Rockies are snowcapped all year round, even in the southern ranges. West of the mountain range are the western plateaus and the Grand Canyon, one of the

Below: **Jackson Lake is the largest of the glacier lakes dotting Wyoming's Teton mountain range. At Grand Teton National Park, the lakes and streams are filled with fish. Herds of wild buffalo, antelope, and elk roam the pine-forested slopes of the range's snow-covered peaks, some as high as 7,000 feet (2,134 meters).**

Left: **Measuring 277 miles (446 km) in length and up to 18 miles (29 km) in width, the Grand Canyon is a gorge carved out by the Colorado River. Its north and south rims at Grand Canyon National Park in Arizona offer the best views. Visitors can enjoy scenic roads, raft rides down the river, and hiking and mule pack trails.**

world's natural wonders. The Pacific ranges run along the west coast and into Alaska, where Mt. McKinley, the nation's highest peak, is found. The west coast is subject to earthquakes. Located near the San Andreas Fault, a major fracture in Earth's crust, San Francisco experienced major earthquakes in 1906 and 1989.

There are six great rivers in the United States: the Mississippi, Missouri, Ohio, Columbia, Colorado, and the Rio Grande. The Mississippi is the longest river in North America and an important artery of trade. It travels 2,350 miles (3,781 km) from Lake Itasca in Minnesota to the Gulf of Mexico, near New Orleans. The Colorado, a rapid, dangerous river, races through the southwest before slowing down at the Grand Canyon. Dams on the Colorado have helped turn the surrounding area into fertile farmland. The Rio Grande forms the border between Texas and Mexico and is also used for irrigation. The Columbia, which runs along the Washington and Oregon border, is one of the world's greatest sources of hydroelectric power. In the past, it was noted for its abundance of salmon, but pollution and the construction of modern dams have greatly reduced its marine life in recent years.

THE REDWOODS

Forests of tall, majestic redwood trees are found along the northern California coast and in southern Oregon. The oldest living sierra redwood, or giant sequoia, is about three to four thousand years old.
(A Closer Look, page 64)

Climate

Climate varies widely in the United States, from the wet Pacific Northwest to the deserts of Arizona and Nevada, from the bitter winters of North Dakota and Minnesota to balmy, tropical Florida. In fact, visitors from almost anywhere in the world would be able to find somewhere in the country that would remind them of home.

Above: **In autumn, the leaves of deciduous trees, such as these in Vermont, turn red and gold. In farming areas, autumn is a time of harvest.**

Four Seasons

Except for Alaska, which experiences severe cold throughout the year, most of the country falls in the temperate climate zone, with four seasons in a year. Autumn begins in late September and ends in December. The northern Midwest is hit hardest by winter cold. Hurricanes are a problem in the coastal areas of the eastern and southern United States, while tornadoes plague the Midwest. Along the western coast, warm Pacific Ocean currents keep the climate mild all year round. Temperatures in the deserts of the Southwest are high during the day but drop in the evening.

Plants and Animals

Due to the variation in climate and topography, the United States has a tremendous variety of flora and fauna. Although many large cities dot the country, there are also vast, scarcely inhabited areas. New England is famous for the striking colors of its trees in autumn, when leaves turn from green to brilliant hues of red and gold. The southeastern regions are known for their beautiful fruit trees. Florida has mangrove swamps filled with alligators. Southwestern areas are characterized by desert-type vegetation. Forests cover the northwestern coastal regions. Perhaps most stunning are the forests of giant redwood trees along the northwestern coast.

The United States is home to many thriving species of animals. Deer live in forested areas, and bears roam the national parks. The bald eagle, however, is a threatened species, and the condor is endangered. Conservation groups have organized to protect them. The indigenous buffalo, which once roamed the Great Plains in large herds, has been hunted close to extinction.

THE EVERGLADES

Many plants and animals make their homes in the Everglades, a huge marsh covering most of southern Florida. Averaging 12 feet (3.7 m) in length, American alligators have broader snouts than crocodiles and feed on fish and small animals.
(A Closer Look, page 50)

Left: The bald eagle is a large bird of prey that lives along rivers, lakes, and tidewater areas. Admired for its power and beauty, the bald eagle is the national bird of the United States.

Opposite, below: Arizona's Sonora Desert is home to many cacti, including the large saguaro cactus, which can grow as high as 40 feet (12 m) and have up to forty "arms."

9

History

The earliest known inhabitants of North America, ancestors of the Native Americans, or American Indians, came from Asia, traveling over the Bering Strait when it was a land bridge some 25,000 years ago. After explorer Christopher Columbus, who was sponsored by Spain, came upon this New World in 1492, Spanish, French, and British explorers and colonists arrived. The first British settlement was established at Jamestown, Virginia, in 1607. In 1620, the pilgrims, early settlers from England, landed at Plymouth

RUSHING FOR GOLD

California was a Spanish territory ceded to the United States in 1848. With the gold rush in 1848, the population grew from 26,000 to 115,000 in one year.

(A Closer Look, page 68)

Rock, Massachusetts. With the help of American Indians, they survived the harsh winters and difficult living conditions.

By 1775, there were thirteen British colonies. The colonists were often unhappy with how the British government treated them, especially in regard to taxation. On April 19, 1775, the Revolutionary War began in Massachusetts, with the Battles of Lexington and Concord. On July 4, 1776, the thirteen colonies declared themselves independent. Under the leadership of General George Washington, they defeated the British army in 1781. A constitution was ratified by the newly formed Congress in 1788, and, in 1789, Washington was elected America's first president.

Above: These men are reenacting the pioneers' crossing of the Snake River, on the Oregon trail. In the early nineteenth century, pioneers heading west could make claims to land by living on and working it as a farm or ranch. They usually went in groups and followed trails that took them through dangerous and unfamiliar territory.

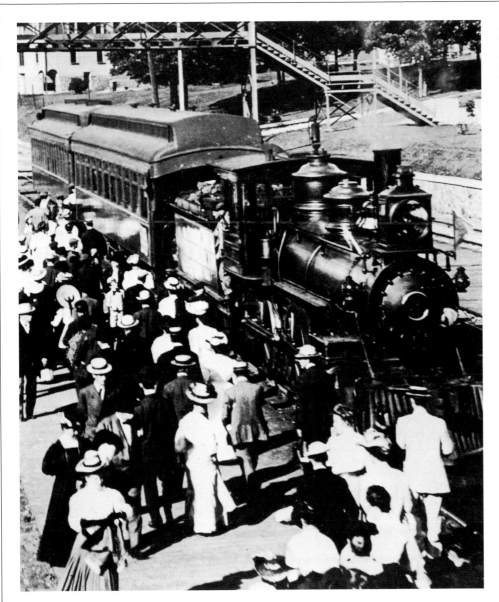

Left: Railroads transporting people and goods to the western frontier were vital to the region's development. In 1862, Congress authorized construction of two railways linking the Mississippi Valley and the Pacific Coast. The transcontinental railway was completed on May 10, 1869, at Promontory, Utah, where the two lines met.

NATIVE AMERICANS

About fifty thousand Native Americans, or American Indians, were killed between 1860 and 1890. Settlers moving west took their land, killed the buffalo the Indians depended on, and brought deadly diseases such as small pox. Forced to live on reservations, Indians were not allowed to hunt or farm and had to subsist on government rations. Keeping their traditions alive has been a challenge for the tribes that survive.

(A Closer Look, page 58)

Westward Ho!

As the country expanded through wars and treaties, pioneers loaded their wagons and headed west. They often clashed with Indians who were unwilling to give up their lands. In 1803, the United States doubled in size with the purchase of the Louisiana Territory from France. Captain Meriwether Lewis and Lieutenant William Clark mapped the unexplored continent during a two-year expedition that took them as far as the Pacific Ocean. America's victory in the Mexican War in 1848 forced Mexico to hand over lands from Texas to the Pacific, including California.

Civil War

By the mid-1800s, the states of the northeast were industrialized, while the states of the southeast were agricultural and dependent on slave labor. Slaves were brought from Africa to work on large plantations, where they were often held captive and cruelly mistreated. In 1861, antagonism between northern and southern states over state rights erupted into civil war. The war ended in 1865, with victory for the northern states. Slavery was abolished, and the nation preserved. More American lives were lost in the Civil War, however, than in any other war in the nation's history.

The country's rapid industrialization in the mid to late 1800s was fueled by a constant flow of immigrants. Transportation of goods and people was made easier with the completion of the first transcontinental railroad in 1869. Shrewd businessmen made enormous fortunes developing new industries. John D. Rockefeller founded Standard Oil Company, and Andrew Carnegie was at the forefront of the American steel industry.

Below: **Although small in numbers, the Confederate army of the southern states put up a good fight. At the battle of Chickamauga Creek in Georgia, the Union army of the northern states was defeated. Soon after, General Grant took command of the northern forces, and the tide turned. He accepted General Lee's surrender at Appomattox Court House in Virginia on April 9, 1865.**

Left: The *Independence*, an aircraft carrier built after World War II, is heavier and able to carry more equipment than earlier models. Newer carriers are also equipped with missiles. Aircraft carriers were first used as combat vessels in World War II, mainly in the Pacific theater.

A World Power

The United States was victorious in the Spanish-American War and, in 1898, emerged with its first overseas territories: Cuba, Puerto Rico, the Philippines, and Guam. When World War I broke out, Americans wanted to remain neutral at first, but the country entered the conflict in 1917. After the war, the United States enjoyed a decade of prosperity known as the "Roaring Twenties." It ended in 1929 with the stock market crash, followed by the Great Depression, a slump in economies worldwide. Increased production for World War II helped stimulate the American economy. The United States entered the war in 1941 and helped defeat Nazi Germany in Europe and Japan in Asia. Because of its size and strength, the United States became a world power with global responsibilities.

PUERTO RICO

The Commonwealth of Puerto Rico was once a Spanish colony. The Caribbean island became a U.S. territory in 1898, following the Spanish-American War. Puerto Rico is self-governing, with a popularly elected governor and a non-voting representative to the U.S. Congress. There is much debate about the island's future. Some want to make it the fifty-first U.S. state.

(A Closer Look, page 60)

The Cold War and Beyond

After the war, U.S. relations with its former ally, the communist Soviet Union, were strained. Unable to reconcile their different systems of government, the two countries engaged in a Cold War, a period of nonviolent hostility. Weapons were stockpiled, and each side was afraid the other would begin a nuclear war. Determined to curb the spread of communism, the United States sent troops to Korea in 1950 and Vietnam in 1965. The Korean War lasted three years and resulted in the division of the country into North Korea and South Korea. The Vietnam War lasted until 1975. It ended two years after U.S. troops withdrew and the communists took over the country. The collapse of the Soviet Union in 1991 brought the Cold War to an end. Since then, the United States and the countries of Eastern Europe have begun a new era of friendly cultural, economic, and diplomatic exchange.

Today, the United States continues to attempt to accomplish many of its humanitarian and economic goals by negotiating with world leaders and providing aid where needed. Since the terrorist attacks of September 11, 2001, however, its focus has shifted to new and complex objectives — fighting terrorism and using military force to bring about a regime change in Iraq.

TO THE MOON

The United States entered the space race in response to advances made by the Russians, who were the first to send a satellite into orbit in 1957, followed by a manned spacecraft in 1961. The first man on the moon, American Neil A. Armstrong, was one of three astronauts on board the *Apollo 11* spacecraft that blasted off from Cape Kennedy on July 16, 1969. (*A Closer Look, page 72*)

Below: The Vietnam War bitterly divided the nation. Many Americans disagreed with the government about why the war was being fought and about the loss of American lives.

Thomas Jefferson (1743–1826)

The son of a wealthy Virginian farmer, Thomas Jefferson attended William and Mary College in 1760. He studied law and entered politics. In his illustrious career, he served as governor of Virginia, U.S. minister to France, secretary of state, vice president, and two terms as the third president of the United States. As president, Jefferson negotiated the purchase of the Louisiana Territory in 1803 from France, doubling the size of the United States. This brilliant man was also an accomplished architect, inventor, naturalist, and linguist. Before he died, however, he asked to be remembered for founding the University of Virginia and for writing the Declaration of Independence and the statute of Virginia for religious freedom.

Thomas Jefferson

Abraham Lincoln (1809–1865)

Born in a log cabin in Kentucky, Abraham Lincoln later moved with his family to Illinois. He helped his father work the land and taught himself to read and write. In 1836, he became a lawyer and earned the nickname "Honest Abe" because of his honesty and integrity. Lincoln was elected president in 1860. One year later, the Civil War began. In 1863, he issued the Emancipation Proclamation, freeing slaves in the Confederate states. Under Lincoln's leadership, the Union prevailed. Five days after the war ended, however, he was assassinated. Lincoln is also remembered for his eloquent speeches, among them the Gettysburg Address at the dedication of the cemetery in Pennsylvania where a crucial battle of the Civil War was fought.

Abraham Lincoln

Elizabeth Cady Stanton (1815–1902)

Elizabeth Cady Stanton learned about the discriminatory laws against women while studying in her father's law office. In 1848, she and Lucretia Mott organized the first women's rights convention at Seneca Falls, New York. In 1850, she joined forces with Susan B. Anthony to publish a newspaper promoting women's causes. Stanton was an advocate of more liberal divorce laws, less restrictive clothing for women, co-education, and the right of married women to control their property. When she married in 1840, she insisted on omitting the word *obey* from her marriage vows.

Elizabeth Cady Stanton

Government
and the Economy

Government

The U.S. Constitution established a federal democracy, in which powers were divided between state governments and the national, or federal, government. The federal government consists of three branches — executive, legislative, and judicial — and follows the principle of "checks and balances," whereby each branch is given considerable independence in certain areas, but its power is kept in check by the other two branches.

Political Parties

The Democratic and Republican Parties are the country's two major political parties. Presidential candidates are nominated at conventions attended by party delegates from each state.

Below: **Bill Clinton, the forty-second president of the United States, elected in 1992 and 1996, delivers his State of the Union address to Congress, advising lawmakers on points he thinks they should consider in their next session.**

The Bill of Rights

Americans are proud of the freedoms assured them by the Bill of Rights, the first ten amendments to the Constitution adopted in 1791. Among the most treasured of these is the first amendment guaranteeing the freedom of religion, speech, the press, the right to assemble, and to petition the government. The fourth amendment protects "against unreasonable searches and seizures" without "probable cause." Since the late eighteenth century, more amendments have been added for a total of twenty-seven. Slavery was abolished in 1865 with the passing of the thirteenth amendment. The nineteenth amendment gave women the right to vote in 1920. The twenty-sixth amendment, passed in 1971, lowered the voting age from twenty-one to eighteen.

CIVIL RIGHTS

Under the leadership of Dr. Martin Luther King, Jr., African-Americans brought to the nation's attention racially discriminatory laws and practices. Their struggle, known as the Civil Rights Movement, had far-reaching consequences for all Americans.

(A Closer Look, page 46)

The Largest Economy in the World

An important factor in the success of the U.S. economy has been its ability to adapt to emerging technologies. Once a strictly agricultural nation, the United States underwent a dramatic change during the Industrial Revolution of the nineteenth century. In the 1870s, the country became a manufacturing powerhouse, going on to lead the world in the production of steel, automobiles, and machinery. At the same time, advances in farming technology made it possible for fewer farmers to produce more food.

After World War II, competition from other countries making cheaper and sometimes better goods threatened U.S. industries. Duties were levied on foreign imports, such as steel from Japan and garments from Hong Kong, to make them sell for about the same price as domestically made products. Even with this protection, the manufacturing sector has declined, and service industries now sustain the economy. In the 1990s and into the twenty-first century, computers have revolutionized all sectors and given rise to new industries and scientific innovations. One of the fastest growing technologies is the Internet.

Above: Keeping manufacturing jobs in the United States is difficult because labor is often cheaper overseas. However, American manufacturers and their foreign competitors have come up with some interesting solutions. At this Toyota factory in Kentucky, for example, Japanese cars are assembled by U.S. workers for the domestic market.

Natural Resources

Another key to the success of the U.S. economy has been its natural resources. The United States leads the world in the production of coal and uranium, used for generating energy. It is the second largest producer of crude oil and natural gas, and its oil reserves are among the world's largest. Water resources have been put to good use — dams on the nation's rivers provide reservoirs of water for general consumption, hydroelectric power, and farm irrigation. The United States is among the world's top producers of asbestos, copper, gold, gypsum, iron ore, kaolin, lead, phosphates, silver, sulfur, and zinc.

Agriculture

Although farming accounts for only 2 percent of the gross national product, the United States is the world's leading producer of agricultural products. It produces enough to provide for its own needs and one-sixth of the world's food exports. About 43 percent of the country's land is devoted to farming. Today, farms are large and highly mechanized and employ approximately 1 percent of the workforce.

COWBOYS

Horse and cattle ranches still exist, but the era of the cowboy is over. In the 1860s, cattle lived in herds on the open range. Cowboys rounded them up and drove them to market. Today, tales of long, dangerous cattle-drives and songs of the brave cowboys are part of American folklore.

(*A Closer Look, page 48*)

Below: **In Idaho, grain is harvested by a combine, one of many American inventions that made farming more efficient.**

People and Lifestyle

More than 290 million people live in the United States. Once a nation of farm dwellers, 30 percent of the population now lives in cities and 45 percent in suburbs, or residential communities outside cities. Suburbs appeal to Americans because of the affordable housing, good public schools, and pleasant surroundings. Many suburban dwellers work in nearby cities and commute by car or train. Nevertheless, a decrease in city populations is creating other problems. Commuters contribute to traffic congestion and air pollution. With deterioration and increasing crime, many cities have become centers for the nation's homeless, a major urban dilemma.

Left: **More than half of today's immigrants to the United States come from Mexico, the Philippines, the Dominican Republic, the People's Republic of China, Taiwan, Korea, and Vietnam. By the year 2050, the population of the United States will reach an estimated 387 million. Of that total, the number of Americans of mixed racial heritage will have quadrupled to an estimated 81 million.**

A Nation of Immigrants

Ask an American where his or her parents and grandparents came from, and they are likely to mention a couple of different countries. This is because the United States is a nation of immigrants. Except for American Indians, who make up less than 1 percent of the population, everyone else belongs to a melting pot of different races and ethnic traditions. The early white settlers in North America were English. Many of them brought slaves from Africa to work the land. As the United States grew, more immigrants came from all over the world. When they first arrived, they often remained in closely knit communities. In New York, there was Little Italy and in Los Angeles Little Tokyo. These places still exist today, but most of the children of the immigrants who settled there have moved into the mainstream of American culture.

At Home

In many homes, the most important room is the kitchen, where food is prepared and served in an informal atmosphere, and where family members often sit and talk. It is not unusual for friends to drop by for a visit. When they do, it is polite to offer them something to eat or drink. On the weekends, many families get together for neighborhood barbecues in the suburbs. Most suburban homes have backyards with plenty of room for parties and guests.

Above: A fun pastime in the rural United States is to hop on the back of a hay truck and go for an evening ride with family and friends through the countryside. This is usually done in the summer or at harvest time, before winter sets in.

Families

Americans seldom live their entire lives in the town where they were born. Most young adults go away to college or leave home in search of work. They may marry someone from an entirely different part of the country and move away. For this reason, nuclear families are the norm, and extended families are rare.

In the typical American family, it used to be that the father worked, while the mother stayed at home and raised the children. With more women in the work force, however, many children now spend their days in day care centers or in supervised after-school programs. An increasing divorce rate has resulted in a greater number of single-parent families and blended families, with parents and their children from previous marriages creating a new family unit.

Growing Up

At the age of five, most children enter school and remain enrolled until they graduate from high school at eighteen. Although

Above: **People who live in large metropolitan areas often congregate at public parks where they can picnic, go in-line skating, or take a stroll with their families or friends. On some streets in major cities, one might see merchants selling their wares and performers, such as jugglers and musicians. Street performers sometimes pass a hat among the spectators, asking for donations.**

American culture stresses individuality, being accepted by the group is important to young people, especially teenagers. Friends can offer support and make life easier, but the wrong company can also create problems, especially for those who join gangs.

As young people mature, they are expected to become more independent. Many parents give their children allowances to teach them money management. As children get older, they are expected to earn their own pocket money by doing chores or working part-time. Another important step to independence is learning to drive. In most states, learner's permits are granted at age fifteen or sixteen, and schools offer courses in driver's education. Then, when teenagers go out with their friends, and if their parents allow it, they can drive the family car. Many young Americans leave home between the ages of eighteen and twenty-one. Some go to college and live in dormitories. Others find jobs and share apartments with friends.

Below: **Americans work hard and play hard. Many enjoy outdoor activities, such as hiking.**

Education

Primary and secondary school education is compulsory in the United States. Most students go to taxpayer-supported public schools, but parents also have the option of paying tuition to send their children to private schools or supplementing classes with lessons at home.

Children attend kindergarten at the age of five, going on to primary school, then junior high school when they are in the fifth

or sixth grades. High school begins in the eighth or ninth grade. Most young people graduate when they are eighteen years old, but a student can drop out of school at age sixteen.

Classes usually begin at about 8 a.m. and end in the mid-afternoon. Students learn reading, writing, history, mathematics, science, and a variety of other subjects. To help children who come from homes where English is not spoken, some schools provide classroom instruction in more than one language. Extracurricular activities are also important. After school, teams from different schools compete at sports, such as baseball and football. Students with special interests, such as drama or science, form clubs that get together after school and are supervised by teachers.

Above: **Kindergarten helps prepare students for the first grade, which most children enter when they are six years old. In the United States, schools are centers for learning as well as sports and social activities.**

Left: Graduating from high school is a big event for students and their parents. For the graduation ceremony, students wear long gowns and caps with tassels. When the high school principal declares them graduates, they move the tassels from the right to the left of their caps.

Among all industrialized nations, the United States has the highest percentage of students in higher education. Thirty-four percent of high school graduates, aged eighteen to twenty-four, attend college or university. Every state operates its own public university system. There are also many private colleges and universities, such as Harvard University, founded in Massachusetts in 1636. Students choose a major course of study and take classes that will prepare them for careers after they graduate. It usually takes them about four years to complete their undergraduate studies. They may continue their studies at graduate schools, where they research a subject and are awarded a master's degree or a doctorate.

Religion

The United States is a country where people of more than one thousand practicing religions live in relative harmony. This is a legacy of the first European settlers, who came to the New World to escape religious persecution and made religious freedom a cornerstone of the nation. The Bill of Rights guarantees Americans the freedom to worship. It also prohibits the government from getting involved in religious matters. Unlike other countries, the United States has never fought a war over religion.

A Tradition of Tolerance

Protestants make up 52 percent of the population and are by far the largest religious group. There are many denominations of Protestants, such as Baptists, Methodists, Lutherans, Pentecostals, and Presbyterians.

About 24 percent of the population is Roman Catholic. The territory that is now the state of Maryland was founded by a Catholic, George Calvert. It was the first colony to establish religious freedom. In the nineteenth and early twentieth centuries, the Catholic population grew with an influx of immigrants from Ireland and Italy. In recent years, large numbers of immigrants

Below: African-American church services are famous for their lively and inspired singing. The Pentecostal movement at the turn of the century gave rise to a black American musical form known as gospel music. The songs are religious and technically difficult to sing because of the wide vocal range and complex improvised passages. Famous performers such as Aretha Franklin and Whitney Houston began their careers singing in their church choirs.

Left: The New England landscape is dotted with small churches such as this one in Vermont. Many of the first settlers, such as the pilgrims, came to the New World in search of religious freedom. One of their first tasks was to build a church for their community. Unlike the grand cathedrals of the Old World, the early churches in the United States were noted for their simplicity and lack of ornamentation.

from Latin-speaking Catholic countries, such as Mexico, have added to the Catholic population in the United States.

Jews, Muslims, and Eastern Orthodox Christians each consist of about 2 percent of the population. In the late 1800s, Jews began fleeing to the United States to escape religious persecution in Europe. Muslims, displaced by turmoil in the Middle East, arrived in the 1950s. Islam is one of the fastest growing religions in the United States. Today, there are about seven million Muslims. African-Americans constitute 42 percent of the American Muslim population. Many of them belong to the Nation of Islam, an American denomination of Islam. They call themselves Black Muslims. Eastern religions such as Buddhism and Hinduism, practiced by Asian immigrants, also have a growing presence in the United States.

QUAKERS AND SHAKERS

Religious sects such as the Quakers and the Shakers have a special place in American history. Persecuted in England, they left for the New World, where they could practice their faith freely. When the United States was a young country, these groups helped set a standard for religious tolerance that endures to this day.

(*A Closer Look,* page 62)

Language and Literature

American English

Soon after the country was formed, Noah Webster, a lexicographer, set out to establish a linguistic identity for American English by writing a grammar and a reader using American models. His rules for spelling, grammar, and usage were based on a living, spoken language. British English, he felt, was artificial and relied on rules that were no longer relevant. Many of the differences between American and British English that exist today, particularly in spelling, can be attributed to Webster.

Literature

Early American writers captured the world's attention by telling their stories in a New World setting. Washington Irving was the country's first short story writer. Edgar Allan Poe excelled at tales of the mysterious and macabre. His poem, "The Raven," with its haunting refrain "Nevermore," is an American favorite. Herman Melville used his experiences as a sailor as an inspiration for his novels. *Moby Dick*, the story of a captain and his quest for a great white whale, is perhaps his greatest work. Samuel Langhorne Clemens, better known as Mark Twain, was a humorist and teller of tales such as "The Celebrated Jumping Frog of Calaveras County." Poet and essayist Henry David Thoreau is best remembered for *Walden*, a philosophical book that extols the importance of the individual and the author's love of nature.

Several twentieth-century American authors have won the Nobel Prize for Literature: Ernest Hemingway wrote about life as an American expatriate in Europe; William Faulkner's short stories and novels were about life in the southern United States; Toni Morrison focused on the experiences of African-Americans.

The Pulitzer Prize, established by American newspaper publisher Joseph Pulitzer in 1917, recognizes outstanding achievements in American journalism, literature, and music. Poet Stephen Vincent Benét and playwright Tennessee Williams are among the prize winners.

Above: **Noah Webster (1758–1843) published** *An American Dictionary of the English Language* **in 1828. He was criticized for using American rather than British spelling and for including technical terms. The dictionary was not profitable, and, after Webster died in 1843, the rights were purchased by George and Charles Merriam.**

Poetry

Important American poets include Walt Whitman, Emily Dickinson, Ezra Pound, T. S. Eliot, Robert Frost, and Maya Angelou. *Leaves of Grass* (1855), a collection of poems by Whitman, urges Americans to appreciate their country's natural beauty and nurture the spirit of liberty. Eliot's most famous poem, *The Waste Land* (1922), is a masterpiece of modernism. Angelou is famous for her autobiographical works about her childhood in rural Arkansas in the 1930s. The poet perhaps best loved by American children is Theodore Geisel, better known as Dr. Seuss, the author and illustrator of *The Cat in the Hat* (1957).

THE MISSISSIPPI RIVER

The lives of nineteenth-century citizens who lived along America's largest river were immortalized in the works of Mark Twain, the pen name of Samuel Langhorne Clemens. He liked to travel and wrote humorous and informative accounts of his adventures in the United States and Europe. Twain's works include *The Prince and the Pauper* and *A Connecticut Yankee in King's Arthur's Court*. *Life on the Mississippi* recounts his experiences as a steamboat pilot on the Mississippi River.
(*A Closer Look*, page 56)

Left: *Rip Van Winkle* is the story of a man who falls asleep for twenty years and awakens to find the United States an independent country. The story takes place in the Catskill Mountains of New York State, where the author, Washington Irving, lived.

Arts

Visual Arts

For a long time, American art was dominated by European influences. Artists traveled to Europe to study and adopted European styles with enthusiasm. It was not until the landscape artists of the Hudson River School emerged in 1825 that the United States had its own identifiable painting style. These artists used European techniques but were inspired by their country's natural beauty. American art came into its own after World War II and the emergence of abstract expressionism. Jackson Pollock, Willem de Kooning, and Mark Rothko were artists who abandoned representational art to show the effects of the physical action of painting. Pollock, known for his large paintings, reportedly flung paint at the canvas, creating a maze of globs and dribbles of color. In the 1960s, artists such as Robert Rauschenberg, Jasper Johns, and Andy Warhol experimented with

Left: **The Pop Art movement of the 1960s began as criticism, by artists such as Andy Warhol (1928–1987), of commercialism in American culture. Using bold, garish colors, Warhol painted soup cans, soft drink bottles, and boxes of detergent and sold them to an enthralled public. He later did a series of silk screen portraits of popular celebrities, including this picture of himself. By this time, he was a famous artist and a celebrity in his own right. Warhol was also an innovative filmmaker who made movies lasting up to twenty-five hours.**

SKYSCRAPERS

Commissioned by Walter P. Chrysler, founder of the American car company the Chrysler Corporation, New York City's Chrysler Building was built between 1926 and 1930. The office building's sleek design is typical of the architecture of the 1920s, and its stainless steel sunburst-patterned spire is an Art Deco landmark.

(*A Closer Look*, page 70)

mixed media, using photographs, newsprint, and discarded objects in their compositions. They often highlighted themes from popular culture. For example, Roy Lichtenstein used comic strip images in his paintings.

Architecture

The world's first skyscrapers were the work of Chicago architect Louis Sullivan. The Prairie school of architecture was developed by his former assistant, Frank Lloyd Wright, who revolutionized residential design. Wright's approach called for big, comfortable spaces and included the surrounding environment in the design. One of his best-known buildings is New York City's Guggenheim Museum, which opened in 1959 and houses an abstract art collection displayed along a spiral corridor. Since then, many styles have flourished in the United States, including the glass-box look and post-modernism, featuring classical architectural elements, such as columns and arches, in a contemporary setting.

Music

Each ethnic group in the United States has contributed to its rich musical heritage. Jazz is an African-American musical form that developed in New Orleans at the turn of the century. The blues, another African-American musical contribution, developed from slave songs. Country and western music originated in the Appalachian Mountains in the 1920s. The people who settled there were English, Scottish, and Irish. Their hard lives were reflected in melancholy songs. Folksingers such as Woody Guthrie, Pete Seeger, and Joan Baez also found inspiration in ballads from the British Isles.

George Gershwin was a famous American composer. His opera *Porgy and Bess* is the love story of an African-American couple. Like many musicians of his time, he was a fan of jazz and popular music. Aaron Copland is best known for his ballet scores inspired by American folk songs. Musical comedies, or theatrical productions featuring songs and dances, flourished in the United States. Broadway is the name of a street in New York City where many famous musicals opened, including *Oklahoma!* (1943), *Westside Story* (1957), and the rock musical *Hair* (1967).

ROCK 'N' ROLL

Elvis Aron Presley was born in Tupelo, Mississippi, in 1935. He achieved his first success with "That's All Right, Mama," a song written by African-American singer/songwriter Arthur Crudup. Elvis's records and concert performances enjoyed tremendous popularity. "The King," as he was called, died in 1977. Graceland, his home outside of Memphis, Tennessee, is visited by thousands of fans each year.

(A Closer Look, page 66)

Left: Jazz musicians play at Preservation Hall, a well-known New Orleans music club. Jazz was originally created for outdoor processions. Its distinguishing characteristic is improvisation. No song is ever performed the same way twice. Duke Ellington, Louis Armstrong, and Billie Holliday are some of the great American jazz artists.

Dance

Square dance, the most popular folk dance in the United States, is for four couples. Dancers are prompted by a caller, who calls out the steps they are to execute within a square formation. The United States also produced modern dance, a new and distinctively American art form. An early innovator was Isadora Duncan, who stressed pure, unstructured movement. Martha Graham used dance to express intense, inner passions. Alvin Ailey incorporated elements of African dance into classical ballet. Merce Cunningham developed "choreography by chance," a technique by which individual dance movements are combined and ordered by random methods, such as tossing a coin.

MASTER CHOREOGRAPHER

Born in St. Petersburg, Russia, in 1904, George Balanchine left the Soviet Union and toured Europe with several ballet companies before moving to the United States in the 1930s. There, he founded the New York City Ballet in 1948. Balanchine went on to become the country's most influential classical ballet choreographer of the twentieth century. His acclaimed works include *The Nutcracker* (1954) and *Don Quixote* (1965). Balanchine died in New York City in 1983.

Leisure and Festivals

Pastimes

Many Americans spend their leisure time at home, reading, watching television, cooking and baking, or, more recently, playing computer games or using the Internet. Outings to amusement parks are fun family excursions. Young people like to go with their friends to movies and shopping malls or to rock concerts. Many Americans also enjoy hobbies such as dancing, gardening, collecting stamps or coins, sewing, painting, or woodworking.

Sports Fans

A favorite American activity is sports. In the colder parts of the country, skiing, ice skating, sledding, and ice hockey are popular winter sports. Snowball fights and making a snowman are fun activities for kids on a winter day. Swimming is a favorite summer activity. Other outdoor sports, such as tennis and golf, attract many enthusiasts. Bowling is a popular indoor sport.

HOLLYWOOD

The city of Hollywood, California, attracted moviemakers because the dry, warm weather made it possible to film year round. Although movies are now made on location in exotic places, executive offices, support services, and staff (including movie stars) are still located in Hollywood and its surrounding areas.
(A Closer Look, page 54)

Team Sports

Football, baseball, and basketball are the three most popular team sports in the United States. Baseball season begins in April and ends in October. Football is played in autumn when the weather is cool. Basketball is played all year round.

Many Americans play these sports and participate in competitions and league games, but many more enjoy watching them on television or at the stadium. Going to a baseball game on a Sunday afternoon is a traditional pastime that is still a special treat. Part of the experience is eating hot dogs, cotton candy, or peanuts.

Football, called American football in the rest of the world, evolved in the mid-nineteenth century from English rugby. Football teams are composed of eleven players who wear heavy protective gear and helmets. It is a rough game, and injuries are common. Nevertheless, it is a standard feature of most high schools and universities. Championship finals between leading college teams, such as the Rose Bowl in California played on New Year's Day, are very popular and attract large television audiences. High school football games are an important Friday night social event for high school students.

Opposite: **Camping is a popular American leisure activity. One of the highlights of camping is cooking your own food over an open campfire without a lot of equipment. This family is roasting marshmallows on twigs.**

Below: **People who live fairly close to the water often go to the beach for the day. They can swim, surf, have a picnic lunch, and play volleyball. Hawaii's Waikiki Beach in Honolulu is a popular vacation spot renowned for its scenic beauty and water sports.**

Baseball

Baseball, the traditional American sport, evolved in the mid-nineteenth century from the British game of rounders. A player hits the ball with a bat and then runs around the diamond-shaped field formed by four bases, touching each base in turn. When the batter comes full circle to reach home base, he or she scores one run for the team. If the ball is caught by a player on the opposing team before it hits the ground, however, the batter is out. The annual World Series is a playoff between the two best teams of the National and American Leagues and is watched on television by millions of Americans.

Little League

Parents usually get involved in their children's sports activities. They attend athletic events at schools, often helping with the cost of uniforms and transportation to and from games. In just about every community, there is Little League, an organization of baseball teams for young baseball players aged eight to twelve.

BASKETBALL

Invented in 1891, basketball is a fast-paced game that can be played in a gymnasium or outdoors. Many National Basketball Association (NBA) players were star players in high school, going to college on basketball scholarships before turning professional.
(*A Closer Look, page 44*)

Below: American children have many opportunities to participate in sports. They can join a team at school or play in community-sponsored sporting events.

Left: Jogging, bicycling, and in-line skating are good ways to get outside and enjoy the fresh air. Many Americans are very health conscious and exercise on a regular basis. Some go to health clubs or gyms to work out, and many look for fun activities that bring them close to nature.

It used to be only for boys until 1974, when girls were admitted. Two divisions for older children have also been added. Little League teams are coached and sponsored by parents. Games are held on weekends and are fun family outings and community social events.

Outdoor Activities

The open spaces of the United States provide the perfect setting for leisure activities. Many Americans enjoy being in the great outdoors and going camping, hiking, river rafting, or rock climbing. The large number of national parks and public recreational facilities are excellent for day or weekend excursions. On Friday nights in many cities, roads are crowded with vehicles headed for people's favorite recreation spots. Some like to "rough it" and camp outdoors. Those who want the comforts of home might invest in a motor home or camper. Others prefer to stay in motels.

Festivals

For Americans, holidays are a time for families to be together. The nation's independence is celebrated on July 4 with picnics and fireworks. Thanksgiving dates back to the time of the pilgrims. After a difficult winter, these early European settlers celebrated their first year in the New World by preparing a feast and sharing it with the Indians who helped them survive. They made dishes using plants and animals indigenous to North America, such as turkey, cranberries, and pumpkins.

Christmas is a Christian holiday celebrated by nearly all Americans. It is a festive time, when families have fun hanging up stockings for Santa's gifts and decorating Christmas trees with lights and brightly colored ornaments. Easter is another Christian holiday celebrated in many homes with parties and Easter egg hunts, which are occasions for children to find colored eggs and chocolate bunnies hidden in the yard or around the house.

Above: **Christmas falls on December 25 and is a public holiday. Many families get into the spirit long before by putting up Christmas decorations and buying gifts. In just about every shopping mall, children line up to visit Santa Claus and tell him what they want for Christmas. They are usually rewarded with a candy cane.**

Ethnic Holidays

Juneteenth is celebrated by African-Americans. It recalls the day in 1865 when news of the abolition of slavery finally reached Texas. Jewish people celebrate Hanukkah by putting a menorah, an eight-pronged candlestick, in the window. A candle is lit on each night of the festival. Mexican-Americans celebrate Cinco de Mayo, the day when the invading French were defeated at the battle of Puebla. Chinese-Americans in San Francisco celebrate the Lunar New Year with the biggest dragon parade in the world. Irish-Americans celebrate St. Patrick's Day by wearing green and having huge parades in many cities across the country.

HALLOWEEN

Jack-o'-lanterns are hollowed pumpkins carved for Halloween and lit with candles. They light the way for children as they go from house to house dressed in costumes and asking for candy.
(*A Closer Look, page 52*)

Left: Thanksgiving is a public holiday that falls on the fourth Thursday in November. New York City celebrates with a spectacular Thanksgiving Day Parade. The rest of the nation enjoys the fun by watching the parade on television.

Food

American cuisine is more than hamburgers and Coca-Cola; it is a reflection of the country's immigrant heritage. The New World offered European settlers forests filled with game. When the pilgrims came, the Indians introduced them to more than fifty new plants, including tomatoes, pecans, and chili peppers. On Thanksgiving Day, the pilgrims prepared a feast that has become traditional: roast turkey with bread stuffing, cranberry sauce, and pumpkin pie. The ingredients were indigenous, but the cooking methods were brought from England by the settlers. Since then, other immigrant groups have added their culinary contributions to American meals.

Mealtimes

Most Americans eat three meals a day. A traditional American breakfast is eggs, bacon, and toast, served with coffee and orange

Below: **A delicatessen is a store that sells prepared foods, particularly meats and cheeses. Many of them have lunch counters serving soup and sandwiches, such as sliced corned beef on rye bread.**

juice. Pancakes topped with maple syrup is a breakfast treat that dates back to frontier days. Most Americans start the day with a light breakfast, such as toast or cereal with fruit. Lunch is typically a sandwich or, perhaps, soup or salad. Dinner is usually the big meal of the day. In many families, dinner is a time for everyone to sit down together and talk about events of the day.

Regional Specialities

New England is known for Boston baked beans (sweet white beans cooked in a tomato sauce) and clam chowder (a soup made with clams and salted pork). Kosher food, or food that follows Jewish dietary laws, is popular in New York City, where many European Jews settled. A well-known Jewish dish is matzo ball soup, or chicken broth with dumplings made from matzo, the unleavened bread Jews eat at Passover. Grits, a dish made from cornmeal, and fried chicken are southern specialities. New Orleans is known for spicy seafood dishes such as gumbo, a thick soup with shrimp, ham, and okra. Texas is famous for chili con carne, a spicy stew of beans and meat. Bratwurst, a type of sausage brought from Germany, is a popular Wisconsin treat. California pioneered "nouvelle cuisine," an approach to cooking that favors fresh ingredients and unusual combinations of spices and condiments. In cities that have large Mexican-American communities, authentic Mexican food is popular.

A CLOSER LOOK AT THE USA

The United States is a country of breathtaking beauty, from the spectacular redwood forests of the northwestern states to the teeming wildlife of the Everglades in Florida. Much of the nation's history has involved a close relationship with nature and the discovery and preservation of this natural heritage. This section provides glimpses into a poignant past: the life of the cowboys on the frontier, the impact of gold on the settling of the

Opposite: **Americans love parades. Just about all parades include high school marching bands and members of community organizations dressed as clowns.**

American West, life on the Mississippi River, and the long, often painful relationship between white settlers and Native Americans.

The past also points to some legendary achievements by the United States. Americans built the first skyscrapers in the late 1800s and put the first man on the moon in 1969. From the Civil Rights Movement to the perseverance of the Quakers and Shakers, the pursuit of freedom and justice is a story told many times in American history books. This liberating spirit has also found its way into national culture and expression — look at the bold steps made by American rock 'n' roll musicians and Hollywood artists.

Above: **In the United States, there are many occasions for face painting. It is a popular activity at fairs and carnivals. Some face painters offer their services for a small fee in public parks on the weekends.**

Basketball

In 1891, James Naismith invented basketball while studying to become a physical education instructor at the Young Men's Christian Association (YMCA) in Springfield, Massachusetts. In those days, students did boring exercise routines, and Naismith wanted a more exciting activity for them to enjoy. He came up with the idea of players from opposing teams trying to score points by throwing a ball into peach baskets set up high.

Basketball caught on rapidly. It was an easy game to learn and could be played indoors, making it an ideal sport for schools, especially in winter. Over the years, the rules of the game were changed, mostly to speed up the action on the court. Women's basketball was first played in 1893 at Sophie Newcomb College in New Orleans, Louisiana. In 1936, basketball was included as an event in the Olympic Games.

The first professional basketball league was formed in 1898. Today, the sport is regulated by the National Basketball Association (NBA), home to twenty-seven teams made up of the most elite players in the world. The NBA has an eighty-one game season followed by a play-off tournament involving the top sixteen teams. Since the establishment of the NBA in 1949, various semiprofessional and professional leagues have sprung up overseas, particularly in Europe, Australia, and Asia.

The Women's National Basketball Association (WNBA) was founded in 1997, partly to bring top female players back to the United States. It has ten teams and plays in a thirty-game regular season. The play-offs include four teams.

Above: **Jordan's advice to young people is: "Don't be afraid to fail, because a lot of people fail to be successful. There are many times that I've failed, but yet I've been successful."**

Basketball Stars

Superstars are not new to basketball. Forrest "Phog" Allen learned the game from Naismith and went on to play and coach at the University of Kansas. One of his players, the great Wilt "the Stilt" Chamberlain, stood more than 7 feet (2.1 m) tall. In 1962, Chamberlain scored a record one hundred points in an NBA game. Even taller was Lew Alcindor, later known by the name Kareem Abdul-Jabbar. A star player for the University of California at Los Angeles (UCLA) in the 1960s, Alcindor went on to play in the NBA, where he led his teams to six NBA championship titles.

Michael Jordan

Michael Jordan has dazzled the basketball world season after season during his long career. Born in 1963 in New York City, Jordan grew up in Wilmington, North Carolina and went to the University of North Carolina on a basketball scholarship. In his first year, he scored the winning basket in the NCAA championship game. In the following year, he was selected College Player of the Year.

Jordan joined the Chicago Bulls in 1984, when he became one of the league's top scorers and was named Rookie of the Year. He was the top NBA scorer for four consecutive seasons and was named NBA Most Valuable Player five times. Jordan also helped the U.S. team win the Olympic gold medal in 1984 and 1992.

Jordan was the world's highest paid athlete in 1998, earning a salary of $31 million and more than $40 million in endorsements. In January 1999, he announced his decision to retire from professional basketball. In October 2001, Jordan returned to the game as guard for the Washington Wizards, a team he had previously partly owned.

Below: Basketball has undergone several changes since its invention in 1891. Peach baskets have been replaced by nets held by hoops. In 1954, a "shot clock" was introduced to make the games faster, higher-scoring, and more exciting. In the 1960s, the three-point shot was adopted. It changed the offensive strategy of the game, making long-range shooters just as effective as tall players who could reach the basket.

Civil Rights

After the Civil War in the 1800s, many discriminatory laws and practices were enacted against black people. In the southern states, African-Americans had to attend separate schools, drink from separate public drinking fountains, and eat at separate restaurants. When they took the bus, they were forced to sit in the back, because the front of the bus was reserved for white people.

On December 1, 1955, Rosa Parks, a seamstress and secretary of the Montgomery, Alabama, chapter of the National Association for the Advancement of Colored People (NAACP), was arrested for refusing to give up her seat in front and go to the back of the bus. The Montgomery African-American community had long been unhappy about their treatment on the city's buses and called for a boycott. The boycott lasted 381 days and ended when the Supreme Court ruled that racial segregation was illegal. In 1956, Montgomery's buses were desegregated.

Below: **On August 28, 1963, more than 200,000 people marched to the Lincoln Memorial in Washington, D.C., to show their support for civil rights legislation pending in Congress. Many Americans watched the event on television and listened to Dr. Martin Luther King, Jr.'s stirring speech with the immortal words, "I have a dream."**

The boycott also helped bring the African-American people's struggle to national attention. Baptist minister Dr. Martin Luther King, Jr. (1929–1968) emerged as an influential leader and eloquent spokesman for racial equality. An admirer of the nonviolent Indian leader Mohandas Gandhi, King led marches and organized voter registration campaigns to demonstrate the determination to peacefully end segregation.

In 1960, four African-American college students in Greensboro, North Carolina, sat down at lunch counters for whites only and asked to be served. "Sit-ins," as they were called, spread throughout the South. They were followed by "freedom riders," black and white, who traveled around the South by bus, testing whether bus stations were following a 1960 Supreme Court decision ordering them to desegregate. Demanding equal rights in education, African-Americans enrolled in schools and universities for whites only. Sometimes protestors were attacked with dogs and high-pressure water hoses. These scenes, shown on national television, shed light on injustice and discrimination and helped build support for equal rights legislation, such as the Civil Rights Act (1964) and the Voting Rights Act (1965).

Cowboys

The first American cowboys arrived in Texas in the 1820s, but their roots go back to the horseback-riding cattle ranchers of Mexico, Chile, Venezuela, and Argentina. *Vaqueros* (vah-KAY-rohs), or ranch hands on large Mexican ranches, wore wide-brimmed sombreros, which eventually transformed into American cowboy hats. They carried ropes, which became the cowboy's lariat, used to catch cattle. After Anglo-American settlers in Texas won independence from Mexico in 1835, Mexican ranchers were forced out, leaving their cattle behind for the taking.

Below: **Popular depictions of American cowboys often overlook their job hazards. Forgotten, too, are the black cowboys, treated equally on cattle drives but not in towns.**

The Texas Longhorn, the main breed of cattle in Texas, was descended from Andalusian cattle brought from Spain by the conquistadors and English cows brought west by settlers. There was so much land in Texas that wooden fences were impractical, so cattle roamed free.

The days of the great cattle drives began after gold was discovered in California. A $10 Texas Longhorn sold for $100 in California, so ranchers began driving their herds over the long and difficult California Trail to San Francisco. In the spring,

COWGIRLS

Cowgirls were women who worked on ranches, helping to herd and look after cattle. Many cowgirls were the wives and daughters of ranchers.

cowboys gathered the herds and branded the calves by putting their owner's mark on their hides with a hot iron. In the fall, there was a second roundup. This time, cowboys separated the cattle to be driven to market. Cattle drives lasted about three months. It took eight to ten cowboys to drive a herd of up to three thousand cattle. Bad weather, rough terrain, and rushing rivers made the drives difficult and dangerous. Cattle scare easily and, when they do, run blindly in a stampede. Rounding them up again could take days. A cowboy had to be skilled in breaking and riding horses, roping, branding, blacksmithing, and taking care of sick cattle. At the end of a drive, he was paid what is today about $75.

In 1867, a cattle-shipping depot opened on the transcontinental railroad in Abilene, Kansas. Between 1867 and 1871, more than one million head of cattle were driven along the Chisholm Trail that began in Texas, went across Oklahoma, and ended in Abilene, where the cattle were shipped to slaughterhouses in eastern cities.

The era of the cowboy came to an end in the 1890s. Barbed wire, an American invention, appeared in 1867, making it possible to fence in the open range. Railroads built branch lines in the 1880s, and cattle drives became events of the past.

Above: **Cowboys still exist. Rodeos are competitions where they test their skills — such as roping cattle and racing their horses through obstacle courses.**

The Everglades

The Everglades is a huge marsh that covers most of southern Florida. Unlike most marshes, however, the Everglades does not lie still. Its water moves slowly over an area of 4,000 square miles (10,360 square km), stretching from Lake Okeechobee to the Gulf of Mexico. A cycle of rain and drought brings an extraordinary richness of life to this area.

From May through October, heavy rains fall on southern Florida, building up in shallow Lake Okeechobee until the water overflows the banks of the lake and begins its slow descent southward. It flows, 6 inches (15.2 centimeters) deep in most places, through fields of saw grass, leaving only a few shifting islands in its path, until it reaches the mangrove estuaries of the Gulf of Mexico. Then the rains stop, and the water recedes. The

Left: **Covering an area of 1.4 million acres (567,000 hectares), Everglades National Park is home to forty-five indigenous species of plants found nowhere else in the world. It is also where wading birds come to nest. Fish, amphibians and reptiles multiply in the nutrient-rich water of the park.**

remaining water is packed with fish, amphibians, and reptiles. Birds, alligators, and other predators come to the pools to feast. Wading birds — herons, egrets, ibis, and storks — come to nest. In the 1930s, 300,000 birds came to nest; the number later fell to between 50,000 and 100,000, and hit a low of 10,000 in the 1990s, as pollution and disturbances in the natural cycles took their toll on the bird population.

At the beginning of the twentieth century, businessmen in search of land began draining the Everglades and building canals, houses, and farms. Marjory Stoneman Douglas was one of the few defenders of this fragile ecosystem. Born in 1890 in Minnesota, Douglas came to Florida in 1915 to join her father and worked for him at the *Miami Herald* as a reporter. Her book, *The Everglades: River of Grass*, was published in 1947 and remains the most definitive study of the area. In the same year, the Everglades National Park was established. Douglas continued her work to increase public awareness of the value of the wetlands. In 1993, she was awarded the Presidential Medal of Honor.

Above: **Now a wildlife haven, the Everglades was once the domain of the Seminole Indians. It was also a refuge for runaway slaves. This fragile ecosystem was threatened by developers who wanted to drain the marshes and build on the land.**

Halloween

Halloween falls on October 31. On Halloween night, children dress up in costumes and go around to their neighbors' houses, knocking on doors and saying, "Trick or treat," hoping to be given some candy. Most American homes are sure to have plenty of treats on hand for Halloween.

Halloween is a very old holiday that originated in the British Isles. For the Celts, it marked the end of summer and the eve of the new year and was considered a good time for predicting the future. On this night, the souls of the dead were thought to come back to visit their former homes. Bonfires were set on hilltops to scare away the evil spirits, and rites were performed to placate the supernatural powers controlling nature. When the Romans conquered Britain, they added features of the Roman harvest festival held on November 1 to the Halloween festivities. The harvest festival honored Pomona, goddess of the fruits of trees.

Below: **Pumpkins grow on vines and are harvested in the fall. They can be carved into jack-o'-lanterns for Halloween or used to make pumpkin pie.**

52

Left: Favorite Halloween characters are witches, devils, ghosts, and monsters. Adults also enjoy getting dressed up in costumes. In the United States, on Halloween, you may see a store employee dressed in a gorilla costume standing behind a cash register!

All Hallows' Eve

When the Celts converted to Christianity, they held on to many of their old practices. October 31 became All Hallows' Eve, the eve of the Christian All Saints' Day. However, it continued to be a night of ghosts, witches, and demons. When the Irish came to the United States in the nineteenth century, they brought with them their Halloween customs.

In America, Halloween became a night of mischief-making and pranks. The spookiness of Halloween has inspired countless horror movies, amusement park rides, and practical jokes. Halloween activities include "haunted houses," hay rides in the dark, and fun games such as bobbing for apples.

The traditional symbol of Halloween is the jack-o'-lantern, a hollowed-out pumpkin with a carved face. It can wear a grin or a menacing frown. A lighted candle is placed inside, and the light makes the face glow and flicker in the dark.

Hollywood

The idea of moving pictures began with experiments conducted by English photographer Eadweard Muybridge. In 1877, Muybridge mounted, onto a rotating disk, pictures of a horse running. Then he projected the pictures on a screen. American inventor Thomas A. Edison and the brothers Auguste and Louis Lumiere in France built on the technology of Muybridge and invented the first cinema machines.

The thrill of seeing movement on the screen drew people to theaters. The first motion picture to tell a story was *The Great Train Robbery*, made by Edwin S. Porter in 1903. Nickelodeons, charging a nickel, or five cents, to see a movie, sprang up all over the country. By 1907, there were five thousand in the United States. The first movies were silent. Sound was a great technological

Left: Grauman's Chinese Theater opened in 1927 and has hosted more movie premieres than any other Hollywood theater. In the front courtyard, cast in cement, are footprints and signatures of more than 180 movie celebrities. New ones are added almost every year. The theater is located on Hollywood Boulevard, the city's main thoroughfare. Its sidewalks are embedded with over 2,500 bronze stars paying tribute to Hollywood entertainment personalities.

invention. In 1927, Al Jolson burst briefly into song in the movie *The Jazz Singer*. Audiences were thrilled and flocked to theaters to see the "talkies." In order to have enough movies for their growing audiences, nickelodeon owners opened their own studios. In 1911, the Nestor Company moved to Hollywood, California, near Los Angeles. Other studios soon followed, attracted by the warm weather that made it possible to film all year round. Hollywood has remained the center of the motion picture business.

Hollywood's golden age was in the 1930s and 1940s, when some of the best movies were made with the brightest "stars," Hollywood's greatest actors and actresses. In the 1950s, however, the movie industry was forced to compete with television. In response to decreased demand, the studios made fewer but more expensive movies, and fewer movies were made on sets in studios. Audiences preferred real life settings, and many movies were made "on location." However, remnants of Hollywood's heyday still remain. Although they are no longer occupied by their original owners, movie stars' mansions dot the Hollywood hills.

Above, left: **Charlie Chaplin (1889–1977) was a silent movie star best known for his comic character, "The Tramp." Like many of the first movie actors, he got his start performing in music halls. His film career began in 1913 at a weekly salary of $150. By 1915, he was so popular he was paid $10,000 a week plus a $150,000 bonus.**

Above, right: **Leonardo DiCaprio (1974–) was born and raised in Los Angeles. He started acting when he was a child, appearing in commercials and television shows. In 2004, he starred in the hit movie *The Aviator*.**

The Mississippi River

Together with its tributary the Missouri River, the Mississippi River forms the largest river system in North America. The river was named by the Chippewa Indians, who called it *Misi Sip*, which means "Big Water." For settlers, it was an important artery of trade and transportation that helped open the West.

The first steamboat was launched in 1811, and, by 1819, there were fifty-nine. Steamboats were popular because they were faster than barges and offered passengers adventure and excitement. However, steamboat travel was often hazardous.

Left: **In his novel *The Adventures of Tom Sawyer*, Mark Twain's hero is a good-hearted but mischievous boy whose pranks are enjoyed by readers of all ages. This illustration by American Norman Rockwell depicts one of Tom Sawyer's exploits. In this famous episode, he tricks his friends into helping him paint his Aunt Polly's fence by convincing them it is a special job.**

Steamboats were made of wood, and fires were common. Rivers were treacherous, and sometimes a steamboat would hit a reef and sink. The average life of a steamboat was five years. The steamboat era did not last long. The Civil War disrupted commerce, and the Mississippi never returned to its former glory.

Mark Twain

American author Mark Twain wrote many books but is probably best remembered for his stories about the Mississippi River. He was born Samuel Langhorne Clemens in 1835, in Hannibal, Missouri, a town on the Mississippi River. His pen name is a riverman's term that means "two fathoms," the minimum depth of water for a steamboat to safely pass. *Life on the Mississippi* (1883) is an account of his days as a steamboat pilot. *The Adventures of Tom Sawyer* (1876) recounts the pranks of a young boy and is based on the childhood recollections of Twain and his friends. *The Adventures of Huckleberry Finn* (1885) tells the story of a runaway slave named Jim, thirteen-year-old Huck Finn, and their adventures as they travel together on a raft down the Mississippi River.

Above: **Steamboats are propelled by large paddlewheels. Once, they were the fastest boats on the Mississippi River. In those days, pilots liked to race each other. Sometimes, speed would cause the ship's boiler to explode, and the ship would sink. Steamboat travel was dangerous for other reasons as well.**

Native Americans

The first inhabitants of the United States were Native Americans, mistakenly called Indians by Columbus. When Columbus first arrived in the New World in 1492, he thought he had landed in the East Indies. Most people tend to lump America's indigenous people together, when in fact there are about two thousand groups of Native Americans, or American Indians, with very different cultures.

The Indians' contributions to the settlers were great. They helped them survive and introduced them to more than fifty new plants, including tobacco, tomatoes, pecans, and chili peppers. When the settlers arrived, they negotiated a series of treaties for the land. However, in the nineteenth century, as more settlers moved West, the treaties were broken. From 1830 to 1840, more than seventy thousand Indians from the southeastern United States were forcibly moved to Oklahoma to live on reservations, poor-quality land set aside for them.

The Plains Indians were made up of about three dozen tribes. They lived west of the Mississippi and east of the Rocky Mountains. To stay alive, they hunted buffalo on horses captured from wild herds and with guns given to them by the settlers. Along with the pioneers came hunters who killed the buffalo for sport. By 1880, bison herds that once numbered sixty million were almost wiped out. The railroad brought more settlers who then fenced off farmland — a concept unknown to Native Americans, who believed no one could own land, only use it. Like other tribes, the Plains Indians tribes fought hard to protect their ways of life. Red Cloud, Sitting Bull, and Crazy Horse are three Sioux Indian chiefs remembered for their wisdom and skills as leaders. In 1876, the Sioux defeated the U.S. Calvary at Little Big Horn River in Montana. The United States retaliated at Wounded Knee in 1890 by massacring almost the entire tribe, including women and children. Sitting Bull was killed while being taken into custody.

This massacre was a turning point, and, after years of fighting, the Sioux and other Indian tribes gave up. There were just too many settlers and soldiers armed with rapid-firing rifles. Some Indians remained on reservations; others assimilated into the white culture. Scorned by the people around them, Indians were called "savages" and felt like outcasts.

Today, an estimated 1.2 million Indians, including the Inuit and the Aleut in Alaska, live in the United States. About 650,000 live on 285 reservations.

Below: **Warriors wore feathers to signify different accomplishments in battle. Smoking tobacco in a pipe was an important social ritual. Indian clothes were made from animal skins and decorated with beads. Along with horses and guns, settlers also brought to the frontier new ways of dressing that some Indians adopted.**

Puerto Rico

The island of Puerto Rico in the Caribbean Sea is a U.S. commonwealth, which means that it belongs to the United States but is self-governing. A governor is elected to a four-year term, as are members of the Puerto Rican Senate and House of Representatives. The capital of the country is San Juan.

Puerto Rico was a Spanish colony until 1898, when U.S. troops occupied the island during the Spanish-American War. Puerto Ricans welcomed the troops, thinking they would be given independence. Instead, the island became a gateway for the United States to the Caribbean and Latin America.

Today, there is debate in the United States and Puerto Rico over the island's future. Some believe it should remain a U.S. territory, while others hope for independence. Still others think Puerto Rico should become the fifty-first state of the United

Left: **Although its $8,000 per capita annual income is half that of the poorest U.S. state, Puerto Rico has one of the highest living standards in the region. About 7 percent of the island's income is invested in education, resulting in an overall literacy rate of about 90 percent. Most children complete at least eight years of school.**

States. Under the current arrangement, Puerto Ricans are U.S. citizens, but they cannot vote in U.S. presidential or congressional elections. Although they do not pay federal taxes, they receive federal aid and U.S. military protection.

Puerto Rico was the home of the Taino Indians when Columbus arrived there in 1493. Spanish settlers built forts to protect themselves from attacks by the English and the Dutch. In the 1830s, the Spanish brought in African slaves to work on the coffee, sugar, and tobacco plantations. Today's Puerto Ricans are descended from a mixture of ethnic groups, mainly Spanish and African. Although English and Spanish are the official languages, most of the 3.8 million people speak Spanish. The majority are Roman Catholic and celebrate Christmas by going door to door singing carols. The island's rich musical heritage is a combination of African drumming and Spanish songs. Puerto Rican dances are lively and colorful and play an important role in local festivals.

During the past fifty years, the Puerto Rican economy has shifted from agriculture to labor-intensive manufacturing. Workers prefer jobs in factories to working the sugarcane fields and coffee plantations. Many opt to go to the United States to find jobs. Today, New York City has a large Puerto Rican population.

Above: **An island in the Caribbean Sea, the Commonwealth of Puerto Rico covers an area of 3,515 square miles (9,100 sq km). Its neighbors are the Dominican Republic, Haiti, and the Virgin Islands.**

Quakers and Shakers

Because the colonies were established as havens of religious freedom, many religious sects settled in the New World. The Quakers, followed by the Shakers, played an important role in shaping American traditions.

The Religious Society of Friends, better known as the Quakers, was founded in England in the seventeenth century. Persecuted in England for his unorthodox beliefs, founder George Fox (1624–1691) once suggested to an English judge that he "tremble at the word of the Lord." Thereafter, Fox and his followers were sarcastically referred to as "Quakers." To escape persecution, the Quakers came to the New World. The colony of Pennsylvania was established in 1681 by William Penn (1641–1718), an English Quaker.

Because they believe that God exists in everyone, Quakers have no priests. At church meetings, the congregation sits in silence until someone is moved by a direct revelation from God to testify. Because they believe in the value of all people, Quakers have been at the forefront of many social reform movements. During the time of slavery, they helped create the Underground

Above: **This Quaker meeting took place in Philadelphia, Pennsylvania, a city founded in 1681 as a Quaker settlement. In 1688, the Quakers took the first public stand against slavery by voting against it within their community.**

Railroad by providing safe houses for runaway slaves in their escape to freedom.

The Shakers were radical Quakers who were persecuted in England because of their noisy worship services. First known as the "Shaking Quakers," the United Society of Believers in Christ's Second Appearing believe in hard work and celibacy. Their leader, Ann Lee, was an illiterate textile worker from Manchester, England, who came to America in 1774 with eight followers.

By the 1840s, there were about six thousand church members. Shaker farm communities were prosperous and innovative. Shaker ingenuity produced many inventions, including the circular saw and the clothespin. Using local woods such as pine, Shaker craftsmen made household furniture that was designed to be useful rather than decorative.

Today, there are about 300,000 Quakers worldwide, with 125,000 in North America. The last remaining Shaker community is at Sabbath Day Lake in Maine and consists of six church members. Although their numbers have declined in recent years, the contributions of both religious sects to American culture remain.

Below: **In keeping with their motto, "Hands to work, hearts to God," the Shakers established communities known for their hard work and inventiveness. Shakers invented the flat broom and were the first to sell packaged seeds for farming and herbal medicines.**

The Redwoods

Stretching along the northern Pacific coast of the United States are California's legendary redwood forests — towering tree trunks topped by a canopy of evergreen branches. Some of these trees are more than a thousand years old!

Often exceeding 90 feet (27 m) in height, redwoods are the tallest trees in the world, requiring a long growing season and a constant supply of moisture, supplied by the coastal fog. A redwood tree takes four to five hundred years to reach maturity. Botanists determine a tree's age by counting the number of rings in a cross section of its trunk. These rings also reveal conditions the tree has experienced, such as fire, drought, or changes in climate.

Found in groves on the western slopes of the Sierra Nevada mountains in northern California, sierra redwoods, also known as

Left: **The redwood is a coniferous evergreen native to the fog belt of northern California and southern Oregon. Redwoods are characterized by tall, clean trunks, because as a tree ages, its lower branches fall away.**

Left: **Yosemite National Park was founded in 1890, largely due to the efforts of John Muir, one of America's first conservationists. El Capitan is the tallest unbroken cliff in the world and a well-known Yosemite landmark. The park is rich with flora and fauna. Giant sequoias grow in the Yosemite Valley.**

giant sequoias, are the largest redwood species. The General Sherman Tree, in California's Sequoia National Park, has a diameter of 83 feet (25.3 m). At 272 feet (83 m) in height, it is taller than a twenty-five-story building! The tree is an estimated three to four thousand years old. Fossil remains of giant sequoias have been discovered, dating back to the Jurassic period some 208 million to 144 million years ago.

Forest Fires

Summer in the redwood forests brings many thunderstorms and forest fires started by lightning. These fires play an important ecological role by clearing the plants on the forest floor and creating space for redwood seeds to take root. Ashes fertilize the soil, and heat forces the redwood cones to open and release their seeds. Redwoods have a spongy bark about 2 feet (0.6 m) thick that protects them from fire. Even if a tree is partially burnt, it can survive. Because they have shallow roots, however, redwoods are easily toppled. A fallen tree may lie on the forest floor for hundreds of years, providing nutrients for insects, animals, and other plants.

Rock 'n' Roll

Rock music grew out of rhythm and blues, a type of music with lyrics set to a strong dance beat and popular with African-American audiences. In the early 1950s, rhythm-and-blues recordings became hugely popular with white audiences. Seeing this success, record producers looked for white performers who could record remakes of black songs. Elvis Presley's career began in 1954, when a record producer signed him on as a white singer who could sing like an African-American man.

Another breakthrough was Bill Haley's song, "Rock Around the Clock," released in 1955. With its driving dance rhythm and contemporary message, it was a hit with teenagers and set the tone for songs that followed. Other white artists who contributed to the early days of rock 'n' roll are Jerry Lee Lewis, Carl Perkins, and Buddy Holly. Meanwhile, audiences for African-American

Below: American musicians often organize benefit performances. Country singer Willie Nelson organized Farm-Aid to benefit farmers. No matter what kind of music they play, most American musicians acknowledge the influence of rock 'n' roll on their work.

artists grew, and musicians such as Chuck Berry and Little Richard gained national recognition.

In the 1960s, British rock bands like the Beatles and the Rolling Stones were extremely popular. In addition, the "California sound" of the Beach Boys and the Mamas and Papas enjoyed a wide audience. The hippie movement spawned a wave of psychedelic music performed by bands such as Jefferson Airplane, Jimi Hendrix, and the Grateful Dead.

African-American artists, however, kept rhythm and blues going in new directions. Motown Record Corporation was founded in 1959 in Detroit, Michigan, by Berry Gordy, Jr., an African-American rhythm-and-blues songwriter. The "Motown sound" featured African-American artists singing melodic songs with strong rhythmic accompaniment. Motown recorded groups such as the Supremes (with Diana Ross) and the Jackson Five (with a very young Michael Jackson).

American rock music continues to feed off its original sources — blues, rhythm and blues, and country — while also incorporating Latino, American Indian, and African music. Since Elvis, rock 'n' roll music has caught on worldwide, particularly in Europe, Japan, and Australia.

Above, left: **Diana Ross shot to stardom in the 1960s as part of the legendary group, the Supremes. Since 1970, she has had tremendous success as a solo artist, too.**

Above, right: Born in the USA **was rock 'n' roll singer Bruce Springsteen's biggest hit album. Springsteen grew up in a working-class neighborhood in New Jersey. In the 1970s, he gave concerts to benefit unemployed American factory workers.**

Rushing for Gold

The California gold rush began in 1848, after John Marshall, a carpenter, found gold flakes in a stream while building a sawmill for John Sutter. The two men became partners and tried to keep their find a secret, but word leaked out, and the biggest gold rush in history was soon underway.

People came from all over the United States and the world to make their fortune. They came by land along the California Trail and by sea entering at the port city of San Francisco on the northern California coast. Many of them profited by supplying prospectors with goods such as mining tools and services. Some miners did not strike it rich at all. Marshall and Sutter died paupers. By 1853, the California goldfields had attracted 250,000 fortune hunters. However, the gold that was easily mined was

Left: **Prospectors often lived in mining camps close to the gold fields. They panned for gold in California's streams and rivers hoping they would find flakes or nuggets. Their method was simple. They scooped up sand and gravel with a tin pan and then swirled the contents around in a basin of water. The lighter particles floated away, and the heavier flecks of gold ore sunk to the bottom.**

gone. Prospectors left the mining camps and established more permanent settlements. Some settlements were abandoned and became ghost towns.

In the 1880s and 1890s, there were more gold rushes in North America, but they were short-lived. Gold was discovered along the Klondike River in Canada's Yukon Territory. The town of Dawson, founded in 1898, was the setting for many of the novels and short stories written by American author Jack London. Another discovery was made in Anvil Creek, Alaska, where the city of Nome stands today. Fortune seekers traveled to the area, and, at the height of the gold rush, twenty thousand people settled in Nome. Today, fewer than three thousand people live there.

In 1902, Felix Pedro struck gold in Fairbanks, Alaska, and the city grew into a commercial center. Seattle, a port in Washington State, was the starting point for prospectors on their way to Alaska, and the small outpost rapidly became a large city. Those who made the biggest profits were not the miners, but those who provided for their needs.

Above: **Miners deposit their gold in a bank in Dawson, a town founded in Canada's Yukon Territory in 1898. Gold was discovered along the Klondike River in 1896, but the rush lasted only a couple of years.**

Skyscrapers

Skyscrapers originated in the United States and were made possible by great leaps in nineteenth-century architecture and technology. The first advance was the use of cast-iron posts and beams that took some of the load off the outer walls so buildings could be built higher. In 1865, Henry Bessemer developed a process to make steel that was stronger than iron. As a result, building heights increased dramatically. The Home Insurance Building in Chicago, erected in 1885, was the first structure to use an all-metal frame and steel beams. Reliable elevators were another technical advance. In 1852, Elisha Otis invented a safety device to prevent elevators from plunging if their cables broke. Developers were quick to seize the opportunity to erect tall buildings on smaller pieces of

Left: The architect of the Empire State Building said he was inspired by the "clean soaring lines" of a pencil. Built in 1931, the Empire State Building was the tallest building in the world until 1973, when it was eclipsed by the World Trade Center, also located in New York City. The Sears Tower in Chicago, also built in 1973, was even taller. Today, the tallest buildings in the world are the Petronas Twin Towers in Malaysia, built in 1997. Twenty-eight years after it was built, the World Trade Center was destroyed in a terrorist attack on September 11, 2001. The center's two towers were reduced to rubble by two Boeing 767 airplanes that had been hijacked and flown into the buildings.

property. Cities such as New York had limited land area, and skyward was the only possible direction for expansion. An economic boom resulted in the construction of some two hundred skyscrapers in the central business district of Manhattan between 1902 and 1929. In 1914, the Woolworth Building became the word's tallest building. In 1929, the honor went to the Bank of Manhattan, followed by the Chrysler Building a few months later. Built in 1931, the Empire State Building was the tallest building in the world for forty-one years. Its 104 stories taper to a point because zoning laws required that buildings decrease in width as they increased in height, so as not to block the light of neighboring high-rise buildings. To speed up construction, beams and posts were fabricated for easy assembly at the site. Construction of the framework proceeded at the rate of 4.5 stories per week. However, work on the building was dangerous and safety equipment scarce. A hospital was located on the ground floor. Of the three hundred workers working day and night shifts, fourteen lost their lives. The building was completed in one year and forty-five days.

Above: **Some of the world's first skyscrapers help form the New York skyline. Today, the tallest building in the world is no longer to be found in the United States, but skyscrapers are still the most characteristic of American buildings. Visible in the photograph above, the World Trade Center's two towers were designed to withstand the impact of a Boeing 707 airplane. Following the terrorist attacks on September 11, 2001, the two towers stood remarkably for over an hour before collapsing under the weight of the enormous burning Boeing 767 airplanes.**

To the Moon

Left: **This picture of astronaut Edwin "Buzz" Aldrin was taken by fellow astronaut, Neil Armstrong, the first man to walk on the moon. They touched down on the edge of the moon's Sea of Tranquility. Aldrin and Armstrong manually guided their lunar landing module to the moon's surface and back to the orbiting command module. Like many astronauts, both men were former pilots and flew combat missions during the Korean War.**

The former Soviet Union opened the age of space exploration with the launch of *Sputnik I*, the first artificial orbiting earth satellite, on October 4, 1957. Four months later, the United States launched its first satellite, *Explorer I*, a cylindrical object weighing 31 pounds (14 kilograms) and measuring 6 inches (15 cm) in diameter. In response to the head start of the Soviet Union in the "space race," the National Aeronautics and Space Administration (NASA) was established in 1958 to promote U.S. space exploration.

On April 12, 1961, the Soviets leaped ahead again when cosmonaut Yuri Gagarin orbited Earth in a space capsule. American astronaut Alan B. Shepard traveled 117 miles (188 km) into space one month later in the first U.S. manned space vehicle, *Freedom 7*. At the same time, President John F. Kennedy announced that, by the end of the decade, NASA would land a man on the moon and safely return him to Earth.

The first series of one-man space flights was developed by the Mercury program. It was followed by the Gemini program, which called for vehicles manned by two astronauts to test new equipment and technology for space travel. Twelve Gemini flights were made between 1964 and 1967. In 1965, Edward H. White, an astronaut on board *Gemini 4*, proved that man could function in space by doing maneuvers outside the spacecraft. The Apollo program called for a powerful launch vehicle with an accompanying spacecraft to orbit the moon and a module for moon landings. During a launch rehearsal for the first manned Apollo flight, a fire broke out, killing the crew. The tragedy delayed the program. *Apollo 7* made a 163-orbit flight with a crew of three astronauts on October 11, 1968. Each successive flight was longer as astronauts geared up for a moon landing.

Finally, NASA was ready to attempt a moon landing. *Apollo 11* was launched on July 16, 1969. On July 20, Neil Armstrong, dressed in his bulky space suit, descended the ladder of the lunar landing module and, as he put his foot on the moon's surface, announced to the world, "That's one small step for man, one giant leap for mankind." He was joined by Edwin "Buzz" Aldrin, while Michael Collins piloted the orbiting command module. Armstrong and Aldrin spent more than two hours on the moon, collecting samples, setting up scientific equipment, and taking photographs. The Apollo program sent a total of twelve astronauts to the moon and returned them all safely to Earth.

Below: **NASA has launched all manned space flights from the Kennedy Space Center in Florida. Visitors to the Center can see rockets and spacecrafts, plus take a tour through the astronaut training facility and the fifty-two-story Vehicle Assembly Building.**

Foreign Relations

The United States is one of the most powerful countries in the world and exerts its influence widely. Although its foreign policy has been to remain uninvolved in the politics of other countries, the United States has often had to assert itself militarily to protect its ideals and interests. In the nineteenth century, it became the dominant power in the Western Hemisphere. The twentieth century saw the United States develop into a world power.

Opposite: In 1982, a monument was dedicated to the 58,132 Americans who died in Vietnam. The name of each one is inscribed on a memorial marble wall. This statue is part of the memorial.

Reluctantly drawn into World Wars I and II in the first half of the twentieth century, the United States has increasingly become involved in the affairs of other countries from the 1950s onward. Fear of the spread of communism during the Cold War prompted American military involvement in Korea and Vietnam. The United States has also participated in peacekeeping missions and limited military engagements, most of them under the banner of the United Nations. As the United States enters the new millennium, and especially since the events of September 11, 2001, it faces new challenges in the international arena. One of them is terrorism directed at Americans at home and abroad.

Above: U.S. President Bill Clinton addresses world leaders at a U.N. summit in 1997. Beside him is the secretary general of the United Nations, Kofi Annan, of Ghana. The president of the United States attends conferences and meetings with other world leaders to discuss economic development and world politics.

Isolationism

On leaving office in 1796, George Washington, America's first president, set the tone for American foreign relations for the next century and beyond: "Why, by interweaving our destiny with that of any part of Europe, entangle our peace and prosperity in the toils of European ambition, rivalship, interest, humor, or caprice? It is our true policy to steer clear of permanent alliances with any portion of the foreign world." Throughout most of its history, the United States has faithfully tried to follow this policy of isolationism. However, the United States also sees itself as the guardian of freedom and has fought on many occasions to protect its interests and ideals.

Leaders in the Early Years

The U.S. secretary of state has always played a key role in foreign relations, advising the president on foreign policy and negotiating with other countries on behalf of the United States. The secretary of state is head of the department of state and appointed by the president with the approval of the Senate. Thomas Jefferson, the

Below: **General George Washington led Americans to victory in the Revolutionary War and served as the first U.S. president. When he left office, he advised Americans not to get involved in European politics. He felt that the countries of the Old World were frequently at war and that the United States had nothing to gain by allying itself with any of them.**

first secretary of state, later went on to become the country's third president. During his presidency, the country doubled in size with the Louisiana Purchase of 1803.

Faced with the forced enlistment of American seamen into the British navy, the United States went to war with Britain again in 1812. The British scored many land victories and destroyed buildings in Washington, D.C. The battle between American and British forces at Fort McHenry inspired Francis Scott Key, an eyewitness, to write "The Star Spangled Banner." General Andrew Jackson from Tennessee rose to national prominence after successfully defending New Orleans in January, 1815. Unknown to either side, however, a peace treaty had already been signed at Ghent, Belgium, just two weeks earlier.

The Monroe Doctrine

In 1823, U.S. President James Monroe stated in his message to Congress that, although the United States was anxious to avoid any European conflict, the nation would not tolerate efforts by European powers to colonize any of its territories. Such aggression, Monroe declared, would be met with military defense, a stand that became known as the Monroe Doctrine.

Above, left: Madeline Albright was appointed secretary of state in 1997, under the Clinton administration. She was the first woman to hold this position. Born in Czechoslovakia in 1937, Albright came to the United States with her family, when she was eleven years old, to escape the Nazis.

Above, right: Born to Jamaican immigrants in 1937, Colin Powell started his military career in Vietnam. He was national security adviser during the Reagan years and chairman of the Joint Chiefs of Staff during the first Bush administration. Under President George W. Bush, he was secretary of state and the first African American to be appointed to the post.

Immigration

The United States has always attracted immigrants from all over the world in search of a better life. During the 1820s, about 500,000 people arrived. By the 1830s, this number had increased to 2.5 million, and by the 1850s, the figure stood at 2.7 million. For the new arrivals, the United States offered land, and American industries promised jobs. Not everyone, however, was made to feel welcome. In 1882, Congress passed the Chinese Exclusion Act. It was the first time that immigrants from a particular country were restricted from entering the United States. This law stayed in effect until 1943. In 1924, the Johnson-Reed Immigration Act was passed, limiting immigrants by country of origin. The quotas favored immigrants from Northern European countries.

Above: **Between 1880 and 1920, 23 million immigrants came to the United States. Ellis Island in New York Harbor was the chief immigration processing center. Here, new arrivals were given physical examinations before they were allowed to enter the country. Those who passed the examination were put on a ferry to Manhattan.**

Conflict

The late nineteenth century saw the beginning of the United States' rapid rise to a position of international influence. Victory in the 1898 Spanish-American War gave the United States its first overseas colonies. Periods of isolationism were interrupted by participation in the two World Wars. After World War II, the spread of communism and the Soviet takeover of Eastern Europe led to the Cold War, a period of nonviolent hostility between the United States and the Soviet Union. The United States tried to contain Soviet influence and the spread of communism. The North Atlantic Treaty Organization (NATO), formed in 1949, was a military alliance among Western nations, with the pledge of U.S. support in the event of Soviet aggression.

Although most U.S.-Soviet maneuvers were diplomatic, the Cold War resulted in armed conflicts such as the Korean War and the Vietnam War. Tension between the two countries also manifested itself in other ways. The race to put a man on the moon was a peaceful rivalry, but the threat of nuclear war prompted the United States and the Soviet Union to continue developing and testing nuclear arms.

Against the backdrop of the Cold War, the United States nurtured ties with other countries. President John F. Kennedy established the Peace Corps in 1965, sending American volunteers to help developing countries, experience international cultures, and promote goodwill overseas.

Below: On June 27, 1950, the United Nations appealed to its members to help the Republic of Korea contain communist North Korea. The United States, along with nineteen member nations, responded. The North Koreans, aided first by the Soviets and then the Chinese, were pushed back to the 38th parallel (the 38th degree of latitude). Today, there is a demilitarized zone along the border between the two Koreas. The war ended in 1953, but U.S. military forces remain in South Korea.

Detente

President Nixon surprised the world when he visited the People's Republic of China in 1972. The United States had not had diplomatic relations with the communist Chinese in twenty-two years. With the help of Secretary of State Henry Kissinger, relations between the two countries were restored. A few months later, Nixon met with Soviet leader Leonid Brezhnev, and the two men signed a series of agreements, including the Strategic Arms Limitation Treaty (SALT). Detente, or the easing of tensions between the United States and its communist rival, marked an important change in foreign policy.

The Gulf War

In 1990, Iraq invaded Kuwait. When Iraqi dictator Saddam Hussein failed to meet U.S. demands to withdraw from Kuwait, U.S. troops led an armed force from twenty-seven nations in a campaign that drove Iraq out of Kuwait.

Below: U.S. President Richard Nixon and his wife, Patricia *(left),* visited Beijing and Moscow in 1972, heralding detente, a new age in U.S. diplomacy. Rather than attempting to combat communism, U.S. leaders opened negotiations with communist leaders to reduce the risks of war. Nixon was aided by his very able secretary of state, Henry Kissinger.

The New Millennium

Since the 1990s, U.S. foreign policy has focused on the struggle to eliminate terrorism. In October 2001, following the September 11 terrorist attacks on the United States, the United States and other nations invaded Afghanistan with the stated mission of finding Osama bin Laden, the leader of the terrorist network al-Qaeda and the suspected planner and funder of such terrorist attacks. Although Pakistan claimed it had determined bin Laden's possible location in 2004, by early 2005, bin Laden had not yet been found.

Even though the United States did not have any evidence that directly linked Iraq to the terrorist attacks, President George W. Bush increased efforts to oust Saddam Hussein from power. Claiming that Saddam had weapons of mass destruction that could be used in a terrorist attack, the United States and Britain invaded Iraq in 2003 and toppled Saddam's regime. No weapons of mass destruction were ever found, however, and the incursion into Iraq and subsequent occupation have been a source of concern for many Americans. U.S. troops remain in Iraq in an attempt to bring democracy and stability to the country while the Iraqi people form a new government.

Above: **In the 1980s, U.S. President George H. W. Bush sent U.S. troops to Somalia, East Africa, where warring tribal leaders had hijacked food and medical supplies destined for famine victims. The troops helped make sure international aid reached the people who needed it.**

Left: **The New York Stock Exchange is on Wall Street in Manhattan, the country's financial center. Because it has the largest economy in the world, the United States frequently tries to influence the policies of other countries by limiting or promoting trade. Despite a recent economic downturn, the country's vibrant economy has attracted immigrants and foreign investors alike.**

Trading With the World

From the end of World War II until the 1970s, the United States dominated the world economy. Lessons learned during the Great Depression of the 1930s led the United States to favor free trade agreements with other countries. By the late 1970s, however, the United States was facing stiff competition from developing economies, such as South Korea, Hong Kong, Mexico, and Brazil. Many American companies moved their factories overseas and to Mexico to take advantage of lower wages and fewer regulations. Foreign investment in the United States also increased dramatically, bringing revenue into the country. These changes made American workers fear for their jobs. They reacted by urging the protection of U.S. industries from foreign competition and domination. Tariffs were imposed on Chinese garments, Japanese automobiles, and German steel.

In the 1980s, recognizing the need for fewer tariff barriers, the United States resumed more open trade policies. In 1989, the United States and Canada negotiated a free trade agreement eliminating all trade tariffs over a period of ten years. Today, Canada is the principal trading partner of the United States. A similar agreement was reached with Mexico in 1994.

The United States is also a key player in the World Bank and a contributor to the International Monetary Fund (IMF), helping to maintain global economic stability.

Helping the World

Beginning in 1948 with the Marshall Plan, which helped European countries rebuild their economies and infrastructure after World War II, the United States has provided large amounts of foreign aid to other countries. In 1961, the U.S. Agency for International Development (USAID) was created to help needy countries, providing them money and expertise to implement national programs that promote health, nutrition, and education. Food for Peace is a special program that provides food to the poorest countries.

The Melting Pot Today

The United States has welcomed more than 50 million immigrants and continues to admit 675,000 every year. The law targets skilled workers and professionals, and offers "diversity visas" to immigrants from under-represented countries, such as Bangladesh and Peru. The immigration act of 1965 stopped favoring immigrants from certain countries, giving preference to family members of American citizens instead. The result was an influx of newcomers from Asia and Latin America.

Below: **Children of immigrants usually adapt to their new home faster than their parents. By attending school, making friends, and celebrating holidays, they quickly become part of American culture.**

Bringing Home to a New Land

Many regions in the United States still bear the distinctive characteristics of the people who settled there. Immigrants often seek out areas where their family members and neighbors have already settled. Thus, certain areas are dominated by particular nationalities. New England was settled by English Protestants, who gave the area their tradition of self-government. They were followed by Canadians, Irish, Italians, and Eastern Europeans. Bostonians today speak with the Irish accent of some of these settlers. The South was also settled by English Protestants. Louisiana bears the stamp of the French who colonized the area. Dutch immigrants settled the Lower Hudson Valley in New York State. Swedes went to Delaware. Catholics from England settled Maryland, and English Quakers founded Pennsylvania. New York City has the world's largest Jewish population. The Midwest is another area of diversity. Many residents of the east coast moved there in search of farmland, and they were followed by Europeans: Germans in eastern Missouri, Swedes and Norwegians in Wisconsin and Minnesota.

Above: **San Francisco's Chinatown started to develop in the nineteenth century, when Asian immigrants arrived there to strike it rich in the gold rush and to work on the transcontinental railroad. This section of town is still a center for Asian immigrants, who feel comfortable here and close to home.**

The great amount of available farmland in the Midwest was particularly attractive to those who had been farmers in the Old World. The Southwest is strongly marked by its Mexican heritage and large Spanish-American population, as well as a strong American Indian influence. California also bears the stamp of Spanish settlements and Latino immigrants, especially in southern California, where there is a large Mexican-American population. The west coast has a large Asian-American population; San Francisco's Chinatown is the largest in the world. By the year 2000, whites became the minority in California, a fact that has caused racial tensions but also contributes to the multicultural character of the state.

Below: **Olvera Street in Los Angeles is the site of an early Spanish settlement. The cobbled street and old adobe shops and restaurants are typical of an early California town. Adding to the Old World atmosphere are musicians playing in mariachi bands and folk dancers wearing traditional Mexican costumes.**

USA

A **B** **C** **D**

C A N A D A

1

Seattle ●
WASHINGTON

Columbia

OREGON

IDAHO

ROCKY
Missouri

MONTANA

NORTH
DAKOTA

MINNESOTA

Yellowstone
National Park

WISCONSIN

2

Sierra Nevada

CALIFORNIA

NEVADA

Great
Salt Lake

WYOMING

Wounded Knee ●

SOUTH
DAKOTA

Missouri

IOWA

Chicago

San
Francisco ●

Yosemite
National
Park

UTAH

Colorado

M
O
U
N
T
A
I
N
S

COLORADO

NEBRASKA

ILLINO

Los Angeles ●

Sequoia
National
Park

Grand
Canyon

ARIZONA

NEW MEXICO

KANSAS

Hannibal ●

MISSOURI

3

PACIFIC
OCEAN

OKLAHOMA

ARKANSAS

MISSISSIP

TEXAS

LOUISIANA

Mississippi

Houston ●

New Orlea ●

4

	International Boundary
	State Boundary
■	Capital
●	City
～	River

MEXICO

Rio Grande

Gulf of

Mexico

5

Bering Strait

YUKON
TERRITORY

Fairbanks ●

San Juan ●

Honolulu ●

Mt. McKinley ▲
(20,320 ft/6,194 m)

ALASKA

HAWAII

PUERTO RICO

86

Alabama E3	Mississippi D3
Alaska A5	Mississippi River D2–D3
Appalachian Mountains E3–F2	Missouri D3
Arizona B3	Missouri River B1–C2
Arkansas D3	Montana B1–C1
Atlanta E3	Mt. McKinley A5
Atlantic Ocean F2–F4	
	Nebraska C2
Bering Strait A5	Nevada A2
Boston F2	New Hampshire F2
	New Jersey F2
California A2–A3	New Mexico B3–C3
Canada A1–F1	New Orleans D4
Cape Canaveral (Cape Kennedy) E4	New York City F2
Caribbean Sea E5–F5	New York State E2–F2
Chicago D2	North Carolina F3
Colorado B2–C2	North Dakota C1
Colorado River B2–B3	
Columbia River A1	Ohio E2
Connecticut F2	Ohio River E3
Cuba E5–F5	Oklahoma C3
	Oregon A1
Delaware F2	
	Pacific Ocean A3–A5
Everglades National Park E4	Pennsylvania E2–F2
	Philadelphia F2
Fairbanks, Alaska A5	Puerto Rico C5
Florida E4	
	Rhode Island F2
Georgia E3	Rio Grande C4
Grand Canyon B3	Rocky Mountains B1–B3
Great Salt Lake B2	
Gulf of Mexico D4	San Francisco A2
	San Juan C5
Hannibal, Missouri D2	Seattle A1
Hawaii B5	Sequoia National Park A3
Honolulu B5	Sierra Nevada Mountains A2
Houston D4	South Carolina E3
	South Dakota C2
Idaho B2	
Illinois D2	Tennessee E3
Indiana E2	Texas C3–C4
Iowa D2	
	Utah B2
Kansas C3	
Kentucky E3	Vermont F1–F2
	Virginia F2
Lake Michigan D2	
Lake Okeechobee E4	Washington, D.C. F2
Los Angeles A3	Washington State A1
Louisiana D4	West Virginia E2
	Wisconsin D2
Maine F1	Wounded Knee C2
Maryland F2	Wyoming B2–C2
Massachusetts F2	
Mexico B3–C5	Yellowstone National Park B2
Michigan E2	Yosemite National Park A2
Minnesota D1	Yukon Territory B5

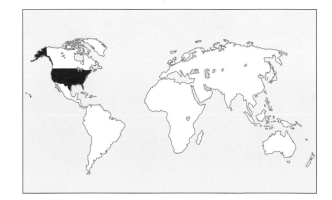

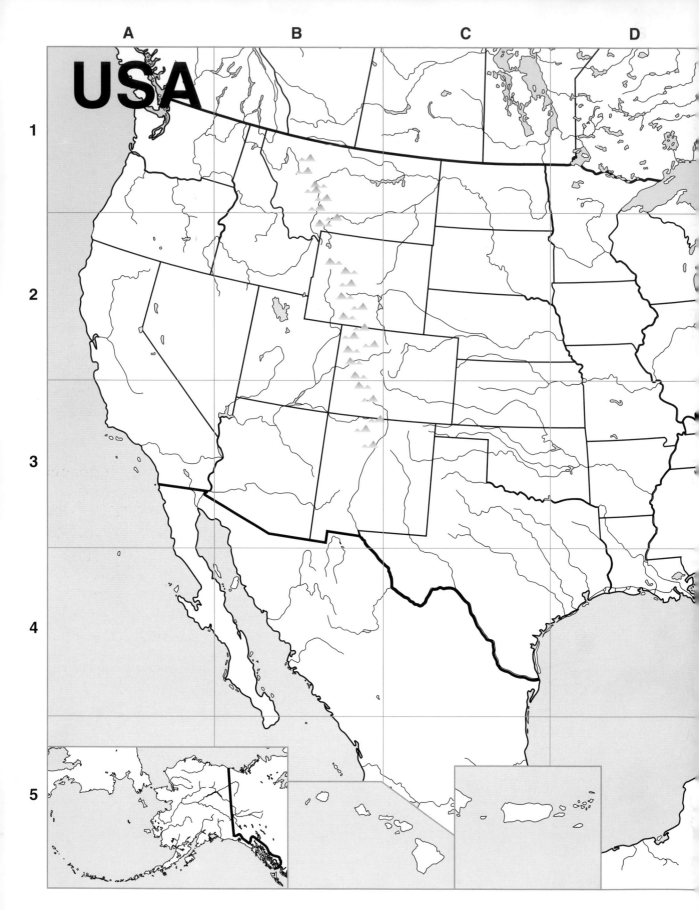

E   F

How Is Your Geography?

Learning to identify the main geographical areas and points of a country can be challenging. Although it may seem difficult at first to memorize the locations and spellings of major cities or the names of mountain ranges, rivers, deserts, lakes, and other prominent physical features, the end result of this effort can be very rewarding. Places you previously did not know existed will suddenly come to life when referred to in world news, whether in newspapers, television reports, or other books and reference sources. This knowledge will make you feel a bit closer to the rest of the world, with its fascinating variety of cultures and physical geography.

Used in a classroom setting, the instructor can make duplicates of this map using a copy machine. (PLEASE DO NOT WRITE IN THIS BOOK!) Students can then fill in any requested information on their individual map copies. Used one-on-one, the student can also make copies of the map on a copy machine and use them as a study tool. The student can practice identifying place names and geographical features on his or her own.

USA at a Glance

Official Name	The United States of America
Capital	Washington, D.C.
Official Language	English
Population	293,027,571 (2004)
Land area	3,787,300 square miles (9,809,107 square km)
States	Alabama, Alaska, Arizona, Arkansas, California, Colorado, Connecticut, Delaware, Florida, Georgia, Hawaii, Idaho, Illinois, Indiana, Iowa, Kansas, Kentucky, Louisiana, Maine, Maryland, Massachusetts, Michigan, Minnesota, Mississippi, Missouri, Montana, Nebraska, Nevada, New Hampshire, New Jersey, New Mexico, New York, North Carolina, North Dakota, Ohio, Oklahoma, Oregon, Pennsylvania, Rhode Island, South Carolina, South Dakota, Tennessee, Texas, Utah, Vermont, Virginia, Washington, West Virginia, Wisconsin, Wyoming
Highest Point	Mt. McKinley (20,320 feet/6,194 m)
Major Rivers	Colorado River, Columbia River, Mississippi River, Missouri River, Ohio River, Rio Grande
Major Cities	Atlanta, Boston, Chicago, Houston, Los Angeles, New Orleans, New York, Philadelphia, San Francisco, Seattle
Major Festivals	Independence Day (July 4)
	Halloween (October 31)
	Thanksgiving (fourth Thursday in November)
	Christmas (December 25)
Famous Leaders	George Washington
	Thomas Jefferson
	Abraham Lincoln
Currency	U.S. Dollar

Opposite: **New England has many villages that date back to before the Revolutionary War.**

Glossary

Bill of Rights: the first ten amendments to the U.S. Constitution, outlining basic freedoms.

boycott: the act of staging a protest by collectively refusing to participate in something.

cacti: the plural form for cactus, a plant found in hot, arid regions. Cacti have succulent, leafless stems and prickly spines or needles.

Civil Rights Act: a 1964 law prohibiting racial segregation in public accommodations and discrimination in education and employment.

Civil War: the war declared between the northern and southern states in the mid-nineteenth century.

Cold War: a time of intense, nonviolent rivalry and distrust between the United States and the Soviet Union.

Confederate: referring to the eleven southern states that seceded in 1860–1861, calling themselves the Confederacy.

Congress: the legislative power of the U.S. government, consisting of the Senate and the House of Representatives.

cosmonaut: a Soviet or Russian astronaut.

denominations: the branches of a certain religion.

desegregate: to eliminate laws and practices that promote racial discrimination.

detente: the relaxing of tensions between nations.

"diversity visas": visas encouraging immigration from different countries.

ecosystem: a natural community formed by the interaction of plants and animals with their environment.

Emancipation Proclamation: Abraham Lincoln's 1863 presidential decree liberating slaves.

extended family: a family with three or more generations living together and which includes relatives such as aunts, uncles, cousins, and grandparents.

fabricated: having parts or sections that are assembled.

federal democracy: a form of government with a division of powers between the states and the national government.

free trade agreement: an agreement between nations to allow trade without any tariffs.

Great Depression: a time of economic crisis throughout the world, beginning with the stock market crash in 1929 and ending with the start of World War II.

grits: boiled, ground cornmeal served as a breakfast cereal or side dish.

gumbo: a chicken or seafood soup with a thick, spicy broth.

hydroelectric power: electricity derived from the energy of moving water.

illustrious: highly distinguished.

immigration: the act of moving to a new country.

indigenous: originating in a particular country or place.

Industrial Revolution: the mechanization of industry that began in England in 1760 and spread throughout the West.

jazz: music originating in New Orleans and characterized by complex rhythms and improvised melodies.

Joint Chiefs of Staff: a group of advisers to the president, consisting of the Chiefs of Staff of the Army, Navy, Air Force, and Marine Corps.

kosher: describing food that adheres to Jewish dietary laws.

Latino: a person or group of people of Spanish-speaking descent.

lexicographer: the writer or compiler of a dictionary.

Louisiana Purchase: territory that the United States bought from France in 1803.

Marshall Plan: an American program to stimulate Europe's economy after World War II.

matzo: unleavened bread eaten by Jews during Passover.

melting pot: a cultural and racial mixture of people living together and forming a combined national identity.

Monroe Doctrine: a declaration by U.S. President James Monroe that the United States would not tolerate military aggression from European powers.

NASA: National Aeronautics and Space Administration, established to promote and oversee U.S. space exploration.

NATO: North Atlantic Treaty Organization, a military alliance of Western nations for mutual defense against communist aggression.

Nobel Prize: an award for achievements in the international community for physics, chemistry, medicine, literature, and the promotion of peace.

nuclear family: a unit of two parents and their children.

persecution: cruel treatment because of one's race, religion, or beliefs.

plantation: a large farm with workers who live there.

prospectors: people who search or explore a region for gold.

psychedelic: images or sounds produced or experienced by heightened sensory perception.

Pulitzer Prize: a prize for achievements in American journalism, literature, and music.

ratified: formally approved.

reservations: tracts of land, usually of poor quality, set aside for American Indians.

"Roaring Twenties": a time of great prosperity following World War I and ending with the stock market crash in 1929.

secretary of state: head of the state department and adviser to the president on foreign policy matters.

segregation: the use of laws or practices that promote racial discrimination.

Sioux: the name used to refer to a group of Indian tribes including the Dakota, Crow, and Winnebago.

stampede: a frantic running of cattle.

Underground Railroad: a series of safe houses where runaway slaves could hide in their escape to freedom.

United Nations: an organization of countries to promote peace.

unorthodox: not conforming to an approved doctrine or philosophy.

vaqueros (vah-KAY-rohs): ranch hands on large Mexican ranches.

More Books to Read

American Peoples. David Murdoch and Elizabeth Baquedano (Dorling Kindersley)

The Empire State Building. Gini Holland (Wayland)

Five Hundred Nations: An Illustrated History of North American Indians.
    Alvin M. Josephy (Knopf)

Minorities Today. William Katz (Raintree Steck-Vaughn)

Presidents. Martin Sandler (HarperCollins)

The Smithsonian Book of the First Ladies: Their Lives, Times and Issues. Edith Mayo
    (Henry Holt)

The United States of America. Enchantment of the World series. Conrad Stein
    (Children's Press)

USA. Festivals of the World series. Elizabeth Berg (Gareth Stevens)

Videos

The American Revolution. (A&E Television Network)

Braving Alaska. (National Geographic Society)

A History of Native Americans. (Schlessinger Video Productions)

Just the Facts: United States Constitution and Bill of Rights. (Goldhill Home Media)

Multicultural Peoples of North America (v.1-15). (Schlessinger Video Productions)

Web Sites

www.georgetown.edu/crossroads/asw/

www.pbs.org/georgewashington/

www.treas.gov/kids/

www.whitehouse.gov/kids/

Due to the dynamic nature of the Internet, some web sites stay current longer than others. To find additional web sites, use a reliable search engine with one of more of the following keywords to help you locate information on the USA. Keywords: *Alaska, American Indians, California, Grand Canyon, George Washington, Yosemite National Park.*

Index

Alabama 6
Alaska 6, 7, 8, 59, 69
Albright, Madeline 77
Aldrin, Edwin "Buzz" 72, 73
alligators 9
al-Qaeda 81
American Indians
   (*see* Native Americans)
Angelou, Maya 29
Anthony, Susan B. 15
architecture
   skyscrapers 31, 70, 71
Arizona 7, 8, 9
Armstrong, Neil A. 14, 72, 73
art 30, 31
   Hudson River School 30
artists 30
Atlantic Ocean 6
authors 28, 29, 57, 69

baseball (*see* sports)
basketball (*see* sports)
Bill of Rights 17
buffalo 6, 9, 11, 58

California 7, 10, 11, 48, 64,
   68, 69
Canada 6, 69, 82
   Yukon Territory 69
Cape Kennedy 14
Caribbean Sea 60
Chicago 70
Civil Rights Movement 17,
   46, 47
   "freedom riders" 47
   King, Martin Luther, Jr. 17,
      46, 47
   legislation 47
   march on Washington 46
   "sit-ins" 47
Clark, William 11
Clemens, Samuel Langhorne
   29, 57

Columbus, Christopher
   10, 58
condors 9
Congress 10, 13, 16, 17
Constitution 16, 17
cowboys 19, 43, 48, 49
Cuba 13

dance 33
Disneyland 34
Douglas, Marjory
   Stoneman 51

eagle 9
education 24, 25, 60
Eliot, T. S. 29
Everglades 9, 43, 50, 51
   Everglades National Park
      50, 51
   Lake Okeechobee 50

Fairbanks 69
families 21, 22, 23
farming 19
Faulkner, William 28
flag 5
Florida 8, 9, 43, 50, 51, 73
food 40, 41
   delicatessen 40
   hot dogs 35, 41
   regional dishes 40, 41
football (*see* sports)

gold rush 68, 69, 84
Grand Canyon 6, 7
Great Depression 13, 82
Gulf of Mexico 6, 7, 50

Halloween 39, 52, 53
Hawaii 5, 6, 35
Hemingway, Ernest 28
holidays 38, 39, 40, 47
   Christmas 38

Easter 38
   Martin Luther King, Jr.
      Day 47
   St. Patrick's Day 39
   Thanksgiving 38, 39, 40
Hollywood 34, 54, 55
   Grauman's Chinese
      Theater 54
   movie stars 55
   movies 54

Idaho 19
Illinois 15
immigration 5, 20, 21, 26, 32,
   40, 78, 83, 84
   immigrants 20, 21, 26, 32,
      40, 78, 83, 84
   laws 78, 83, 84
   melting pot 5, 83
Industrial Revolution 18
industries 18, 78, 82
Irving, Washington 29

Jordan, Michael 44, 45

Kansas 44, 49
Kentucky 15
King, Martin Luther, Jr. (*see*
   Civil Rights Movement)

leisure 5, 21, 23, 24, 34, 35,
   36, 37
Lewis, Meriwether 11
London, Jack 69
Los Angeles 21, 34, 41, 85
Louisiana 44, 77, 84
Louisiana Purchase 77, 84

Maine 6
Marshall Plan 83
Massachusetts 10, 44
Mexico 6, 7, 11, 27, 82
Minnesota 7, 8

Monroe Doctrine 77
mountains 6, 7, 65
  Appalachian Mountains 6
  Mt. McKinley 7
  Rocky Mountains 6, 58
  Sierra Nevada 64, 65
  Teton Range 6
Metropolitan Museum of
  Art 31
music 26, 32, 66, 67
  composers 32
  gospel music 26
  jazz 32
  Nelson, Willie 66
  Presley, Elvis 32, 66
  rhythm and blues 67
  rock 'n' roll 32, 66
  Ross, Diana 67
  Springsteen, Bruce 67

national parks 6, 7, 50, 51, 65
Native Americans 10, 11, 21,
  38, 40, 56, 58, 59
  Aleut 59
  art 58
  Chippewa 56
  Inuit 59
  Plains 58
  reservations 58, 59
  Seminole 51
  Sioux 59
  Taino 61
  Wounded Knee 59
NASA 72
Nevada 8
New England 9, 27, 41
New Jersey 67
New Mexico 6
New Orleans 32, 44, 77
New York City 21, 31, 39, 61,
  70, 71, 81, 82, 85
  Little Italy 21
New York State 85
North Atlantic Treaty
  Organization (NATO) 79
North Carolina 44, 47

North Dakota 8

Oklahoma 58
  Indian reservations 58, 59
Oregon 7, 64

Pacific Ocean 6, 8, 11
parades 39, 43
Pennsylvania 62
pilgrims 10, 27, 38, 40
Poe, Edgar Allan 28
poets 29
population 20
Powell, Colin 77
presidents
  Clinton, Bill 16, 75
  Jefferson, Thomas 15, 77
  Kennedy, John F. 72, 79
  Lincoln, Abraham 15
  Monroe, James 77
  Nixon, Richard 44, 47, 80
  Washington, George 10, 76
Puerto Ricans 61
Puerto Rico 13, 60, 61

railroad 11, 12, 49
redwoods 7, 9, 43, 64, 65
  giant sequoias 65
religion 26, 27, 43, 62, 63
  Quakers 27, 43, 62
  Shakers 27, 43, 62, 63
rivers
  Colorado 7
  Columbia 7
  Mississippi 7, 29, 56, 57
  Missouri 7
  Ohio 7
  Rio Grande 7
"Roaring Twenties" 13

San Francisco 5, 7, 48, 68, 84
  Chinatown 84
San Juan 60
Seattle 69
skyscrapers 31, 43, 70, 71
slavery 12, 17, 62

space exploration 14, 72, 73
sports 24, 34, 35, 36, 44, 45
  baseball 24, 35, 36
  basketball 35, 44, 45
  football 24, 35
Stanton, Elizabeth Cady 15
"The Star Spangled
  Banner" 77
Strategic Arms Limitation
  Treaty (SALT) 80
suburbs 20, 21

Tennessee 32
terrorism 14, 70, 71, 75, 81
Texas 7, 11, 46
Titanic 55
Twain, Mark (see Clemens,
  Samuel Langhorne)

United Nations 75, 79

Vermont 8, 27
Virginia 12, 15

Warhol, Andy 30
wars
  Afghanistan 81
  Civil War 12, 15, 46, 48, 57
  Cold War 14, 75, 79, 81
  Gulf War 80
  Iraq 14, 80–81
  Korean War 14, 72, 75, 79
  Mexican War 11
  Revolutionary War 10
  Spanish-American War 13,
    60, 78
  on terrorism 14, 81
  Vietnam War 14, 75, 79
  War of 1812 77
  World War I 13, 78
  World War II 13, 30, 78,
    82, 83
Washington, D.C. 17, 46, 75
Webster, Noah 28
Whitman, Walt 29
World Trade Center 70, 71, 81